How to be Human

How to be Human

Stuart Murray

ISBN-13: 9781540589460
ISBN-10: 1540589463

"We are far more united and have far more in common, than that which divides us."

Jo Cox MP, England

Contents

How to be Human

Preface

One of my earliest memories is from 1973 when I was three years old. I was on a summer holiday with my family in Caister-on-sea. One night, whilst walking through an avenue of trees draped in fairy lights, I looked up and for the first time saw the stars twinkling in the blackness above. Until then I had thought that stars were pretend. I was so excited to see they were real and remember shouting, "Mum! Dad! Look, there are stars!" The crisp air seemed full of magic and there was a tangible sense of being part of something big, something wonderful.

All children are naturally inquisitive and fascinated by everything. For some reason this philosophical nature all too often ebbs away but for others, as in my case, it remains intact. Whereas most people seem able to just get on with life, I have somewhat found myself on the periphery asking questions like, 'What's going on?', 'Who's in charge?' and 'What's the point, exactly?'

The main thing which has fuelled my desire to understand is people. Like many, I have often found myself upset by others actions, be it someone I have known personally or someone on the news, in a different part of the world. I grew to realise that if I could figure out why people are the way they are, perhaps I may get less upset in future.

By late 2004 I found myself surrounded by many scraps of paper listing my thoughts, ideas, observations, and summaries of things that I had read. At the time I was running my own business which, due to a lack of sales, gave me an opportunity to pursue other interests. I decided to write a book which would bring all this information together in an attempt to try to make sense of it. The overall structure to my thinking was this: how can we know how to behave if we know nothing about who we are, what we are, or what it is we are a part of?

In January 2005 I put pen to paper and completed writing my first version of the book by May 2007. My intention had been to write a kind of instruction manual using reason to explain, at a fundamental level, the best way for us to conduct ourselves. I am pleased to say that what came out went much further. Drawing on some clever scientific experiments which began at the dawn of the Millennium, *How to be Human* shows how each of us can increase our day-to-day feeling of happiness.

I cannot overstate what an ardent rationalist I have been throughout my life. Science has been my religion over the years and I have had little time for phenomena falling outside of it. However, in September 2008 my view began to change radically. Samuel, our beautiful 14-month-old son, was diagnosed with a rare form of leukaemia. He was immediately put onto six months of intensive chemotherapy and we moved into Addenbrooke's Hospital for most of that time. During our stay there we mixed with other children who, like Samuel, were often described by their families and nurses as special. By special I mean, unusually mature and wise for their age; qualities that some believe are attributable to serious illness. This was not our belief and was certainly not the case with Samuel. From the age of just one month people often commented that he seemed like an adult in a baby's body.

Unfortunately, Sam didn't make it. He died in my arms, at home, aged 20 months old. Needless to say this was the most devastating time of our lives; the crushing feeling of loss not something I would wish upon my worst enemy. That being said, the experience taught us much and caused us to see life very differently. As a consequence I wanted to reflect this change of view in my writing, so between 2009 and 2010 the book underwent a rewrite and edit. I realised science does not provide all the answers and decided to leave room for peoples own beliefs around the core message. (I talk about Samuel and the personal beliefs he has led us to have in the chapter 'Do you believe in God?') The result, I hope, is something that people from all backgrounds and belief systems will benefit from.

Introduction

I t is 10:30 a.m. Tuesday, 4th January 2005. Today is the first day back at work after the Christmas holidays for most people in England. If you celebrate Christmas and live in the West then no doubt, like me, you ate too much, drank too much, and as a result spent too much throughout the festivities. But this Christmas was very different, for at 12:59 a.m. GMT, on Sunday, 26th December 2004, one of the worst ever earthquakes struck just off the coast of Indonesia causing a tsunami wave to take the lives of around 130,000 people. Many more fatalities were expected during the coming months.

Amidst the terror, tragedy, and devastation that this gargantuan disaster unleashed upon the world, perhaps rather surprisingly a bright light shone in some of the affected countries. Terrorist groups, which had been perpetrators of death and hatred before the disaster, laid down their weapons and worked alongside their fellow citizens in a new, united cause. Political and religious differences became irrelevant as people desperately struggled to stay alive. Across the globe, governments were rendered irrelevant as the people of each nation led the way in the huge humanitarian response which followed. It was as if the disaster pushed a reset button. Politics, religion, and nationality were swept aside, allowing humans to offer the hand of friendship, unencumbered, to their fellow human beings.

The positive consequence of this terrible disaster was to remind us of something we all too often forget about: our commonality. For regardless of our religious or political beliefs, our nationality or our profession, we are all united by one indisputable fact: we are all human beings.

Before Christmas the news was dominated, as always, with stories of humans killing humans in various different parts of the world. Throughout history we have demonstrated an ability to get along with each other about as harmoniously as a bonfire in a fireworks factory. World War I, World War II, The Holocaust, civil war and terrorism; atrocious events from just recent history alone. Many agree that religion, politics, race, and territorial disputes are the frequent causes of conflict, but even in countries not ravaged by war, like England, there is still violent crime, family feuds, disputes between people at work, fights in schools, and bust-ups between friends. Why is it that if you place any group of people together it seems only a matter of time before something kicks off? Is there something inherent within humans preventing us from getting along with each other?

Like all living organisms, the human biological objective is to stay alive and reproduce. To ensure this, we have a default setting that is basically selfish and insular in nature i.e. 'I must survive and rear my children at any cost'. Despite these seemingly antisocial characteristics, humans, like some other species, grew to realise they had a better chance of survival by living together as part of a group. Things like hunting are more successful with two or more of you, and a group can better protect itself from predators. So, societies established themselves, formed if you like, out of each individual's selfish desire to survive.

Throughout mankind's history our default setting has driven us to subconsciously ask, 'Am I surviving okay?' and, 'What do I need to do to improve my chances of survival?' Societies formed as a part of this continual evaluation of our welfare. Today, many of us are lucky and do not have to worry much about surviving. The society we are a part of takes care of itself, the sense of being part of a community no longer at the forefront of our minds. But nature still drives us to start from the standpoint of ourselves; our personal welfare will always be the top priority. Because of this, questions concerning our survival or survival of the group have been replaced by questions such as, 'Am I happy?' and, 'What can I do to make myself happier?' We believe we can survive perfectly well by ourselves so, for many, thoughts concerning 'I' are those that prevail. Nature gave us survival attributes which today are largely redundant. Unfortunately these have now manifested themselves as selfish, insular, and thoughtless behaviour, without doubt the most common causes of petty disputes.

You could argue, of course, why not be selfish and get exactly what you want out of life? Well, there is nothing stopping you but the key is in weighing the short-term gain of your actions with the long-term gain. It might be nice to always eat the last cake at parties, but if word gets around you could forfeit future invitations (and more cakes!). Could your short-term pleasure result in long-term misery later? Would you be upset by a friend's actions if his behaviour towards you was the same as your behaviour towards him? How do you think you are perceived by others? These are the sorts of questions that, if asked more often, would probably eradicate petty arguments altogether.

So, our default setting may contribute to minor disputes but what about the really serious stuff at the other end of the spectrum? What about wars, terrorism, and so on? Could our biological make-up be in anyway responsible for mass conflict and hatred in the world?

The formation of societies is a bit like individual drops of water running into one another to form a puddle. You start off with isolated, or insular, drops and end up with an isolated, or insular, puddle. Once a group of people come together, those default human settings permeate throughout until you end up with a selfish, insular society. The survival of the group becomes the top priority, for if your community should perish so, too, may you. Living within an insular society breeds a resilience to change amongst its members. Things not understood, things outside the society and your own experience, often becoming feared. Imagine what happened when an ancient community on one side of a wood bumped into another community on the other side of the wood. It would be like two animals rearing up to one another, fearful and inclined to fight over limited resources or a more favourable environment. And, unfortunately, our natural tendency to think within only the scope of the society of which we are a part (our own particular culture), our deluded perception of us and them, is compounded by two natural consequences of societies themselves.

Rules are required in any group if its members are to benefit from being a part of it. Without them there is no harmony, no cohesion and effectively no group. So, the members of a society establish their own way of doings things, their own way of living together, perhaps unique to them. Unfortunately, if the *politics* of one society differs from that of another, it reinforces the misperception of two completely separate and irreconcilable societies.

As humans evolved and became increasingly intelligent they started to ask philosophical questions like, 'How did everything come to be here?', 'Is there a reason for our existence?', 'What is death?' and so on. Perhaps questions like this are inevitable once a certain level of intelligence is reached. Gods were believed to answer such enigmas and are thought today by some to be a kind of extension of our mother and father, those responsible for creating and nurturing us. (Certainly, religions often refer to God as 'Father'.) Each society established their own gods and incorporated them into myths to explain the world around them. Human intelligence brought forth philosophical questions at which point gods, myths, and superstitions evolved by way of answers. These naturally occurring beliefs became entwined with ethics forming the elements of what came to be known as religion. Religion too is, therefore, a natural product of societies. Unfortunately, and as with politics, when the religion of one society differs from that of another, it reinforces the misperception of separate and irreconcilable societies.

So, yes, our biological make-up, the powerful will to survive at all costs embedded in every human, is partly responsible for the conflict and hatred in our world today. It drove us to form closed societies, the moment the seeds of conflict were sown. Each society developed its own politics and religion, two naturally occurring belief systems that exacerbate our misperception of societies as separate and irreconcilable. Of course, these problems were not immediately apparent. Initially, we benefited from living within our own insular societies until, that is, we discovered one another living on opposite sides of the wood. It was only then that the problems began.

Currently we are at a stage in our evolution comparable to the time before societies existed. Instead of isolated drops of water that would benefit from forming a puddle, our world consists of isolated puddles that would benefit from forming a lake. But how does the reality of all this actually pan out with societies today?

The evolution of religion, combined with our turbulent history, has made our world more complicated than my puddle/lake analogy implies. Unfortunately, each of the main religions fragmented into many different denominations with each effectively a variant of the original belief system. (There are currently more than 40,000 denominations of Christianity alone!) The result was societies forming within societies and, to pick up my analogy again, many, many more puddles coexisting alongside one another. Mankind's history is responsible for where these puddles exist today. A map of the world can reveal how some of the worst trouble spots are areas where different society types now live in close proximity of one another; places such as Israel and Palestine, Iraq, and Northern Ireland (although the road to peace now looks very encouraging).

In the same way disputes between friends often emanate from our selfish and insular nature, so too can disputes between different societies and countries. Human evolution has resulted in us thinking first of ourselves, then within the bounds of our society and then within the bounds of our country. Whole nations upset other nations because of their selfish and insular conduct. Whilst putting your own country first may raise your popularity with the electorate, countries, just like individuals and societies, need to consider the long-term consequences of their actions.

Unfortunately, religion has done little to harmonise different societies and paste over this tendency for people to put their own community first. On the contrary, like many, I believe it has actually worsened interrelations. The problem is that humans' selfish and insular nature, our fear of things outside our own society and understanding, found its way into religion (and politics). I believe this is why faiths are so damning of one another. Followers of some faiths are led by religious doctrine to believe they are superior to everyone outside their faith, that they are the children of God chosen to spread his word. People of other faiths, or of no faith, are living their lives the wrong way. They are ungodly sinners. They are a blight on society and must be converted or, worse still, and as some extremists believe, be eliminated.

Clearly, teachings of this kind are not exactly conducive to good intersociety relations. The religions of the world evolved out of different societies and absorbed the insular nature of those societies. Unfortunately, this has resulted in religions themselves being insular and, in some cases, dogmatic belief systems.

Holy books are central to the teaching of each faith and purport that they are, without doubt, the actual word of God. Anyone daring to question a religion's ideology are questioning God and committing blasphemy. But are these books the *actual* word of God?

Biblical scholars have known for a long time that the four books of Moses were not in fact written by Moses but by four different authors, each with their own political agenda. Similarly, they have known for a long time that the Gospels according to Matthew, Mark, Luke and John were neither written by Jesus's disciples or, indeed, anyone who actually knew him. The real authors wrote the Gospels around 70–100 AD, they too having their own political agenda. In addition, it is believed that in order to facilitate control over their empire the Romans distorted Christianity before propagating it throughout Europe. Jesus's original message – one of love, forgiveness, and non-violence to all – did certainly not seem very high on their agenda. The philosophers Baruch Spinoza (1632–1677) and Thomas Paine (1737–1809) were possibly the first people to question the authenticity of the Bible and were both persecuted for the rest of their lives as a result.

The Qur'an, which is, of course, a derivative of the Bible, has in recent times been distorted by the puritanical

Government of Saudi Arabia. It is a tragedy that this intolerant, vengeful and prejudiced version of Islam, *far removed from the original teachings of Mohammed*, has been spread around the world. (There are estimates that the Saudi Government spent in excess of 100 billion US dollars over 20 years propagating their version of Islam.) The fact is that God's word, unfortunately, has all too often been modified throughout history.

Holy books are still very much at the heart of world politics today. They are supposedly the definitive books on how God says we should conduct ourselves as human beings. The core philosophies they teach are of definite benefit to society and, indeed, are sorely needed in our world today. However, the selfish, controlling, and prejudiced politics of man, not God, entwined within these different texts, most definitely is not.

The French philosopher René Descartes (1596 - 1650) passionately believed that we should never blindly accept what we are told. Human history has proved this to be a very sound philosophy. Blindly accepting what someone tells you, whether it is a friend, associate, family member, newspaper, or book can lead to all sorts of problems. It is imperative that we ask questions and research things for ourselves, for only by so doing can we express what *we* truly believe. We must look at all situations with an open mind and be tolerant of other people's beliefs, including opinions generally regarded as deplorable by most (providing they remain as opinions and are not acted upon to the detriment of others). Each and every single one of us has the right to form our own world view, but we do not have the right to impose that view on others. And whilst it is fine to be passionate about that in which we believe, we should allow for the possibility of being wrong. It is by no means foolish to admit when we are wrong, but it is foolish not to accept that we could be. Only by constant re-evaluation of our beliefs can we ensure they reflect the changing world and societies in which we live.

Unfortunately, asking someone who is devout to re-evaluate what they believe in often falls at the first fence. This is one of the reasons that the world has been in a mess for such a long time, many refusing point-blank to compromise their views (which often actually transpire to be man's, not God's, views). We are at a stage in our social evolution where we *absolutely must* take a look at our beliefs if we are to ever stand any chance of living together in peace.

Why do people have such a problem questioning their faith? The Oxford dictionary definition of the word faith is *unquestioning confidence*. If you take this definition literally, I guess my question makes no sense; faith (religion) by its very nature is unquestioning. So instead let's pick up on the second word in the definition, *confidence*. As already said, how confident can anyone be that books purporting to be the word of God are indeed the word of God? It is an incredible claim, and personally I would not want to be answerable to my creator should I have misquoted him/her in anyway. The fact of the matter is that we cannot be confident that any holy books are the word of God. We cannot even be sure that God exists or what God is exactly. (This is explored in the chapter 'Do you believe in God?')

The belief that you cannot possibly question your faith because your faith is God's word cleverly nips questions in the bud before they have a chance to form. However, I believe this is a bending of the truth and is misleading. Those who question the authenticity of a holy book are merely questioning the people who penned, edited, and presented the book in its current form. Questioning the writers of a book is not the same thing as questioning God. Therefore, people should not be afraid to do so. And anyway, wouldn't God advocate the search for truth?

Believing that to question your faith is to question God is not the only reason people find it hard to question their faith. Children brought up in religious families have had beliefs and sacraments central to their lives from the outset; their family life often based around their religion. Growing up within a loving, religious, environment ensures that your faith becomes integral to you as a person. It forms an important part of your personality in the same way that it helped form your parents, their parents, and their parents before them. In later years, the mere act of reflecting upon your religion may evoke fond memories of your family and childhood; emotions, sensations, and smells perhaps come flooding back. It is no surprise, therefore, that to question your faith is to question yourself, your family, and the society of which you are a part.

Clearly this is no mean feat for anyone, whether religious or not.

In addition to the almost inextricable link which forms between religion and family there are at least two other things that make it hard for some people to question their faith. Firstly, it is known that young children are actually biologically predisposed to believe their elders. This is an effective survival attribute as it ensures parents and guardians can rapidly administer instructions in dangerous situations, avoiding children engaging in debates which see them get eaten by bears, for example! On the downside, doctrine instilled into young children can stay with them for the rest of their lives. In the most extreme cases, highly negative doctrine has caused permanent psychological damage, impeding or ruining people's lives. Because of this, we must be very careful what we teach our children. A second obstacle frequently preventing people from questioning their faith is fear. Religion and God provide many with a great source of comfort. The prospect that your beliefs may not be based on the truth is too much for some to contemplate. This in itself is enough to prevent people from wanting to ask questions.

So, clearly it is very difficult to question your faith, but without doing so what alternative is there when you consider the hatred and violence that exist in our world today as a result of current beliefs? Generation after generation has not dared question their faith and generation after generation has succumbed to the same ignorance, intolerance, and hatred as their forefathers. Violence has bred violence and hatred has bred hatred. Societies accustomed to a culture of violence seem unable to break the chain. The time for us humans to take a step back and see the bigger picture is long overdue.

The Greek philosopher Aristotle (384–322 BC) said, '*The fate of empires depends on the education of the youth*'; the driving force behind his massive contribution to modern thinking being, *the search for truth*. If we live our lives according to a system of false truths, how can we possibly hope to conduct ourselves properly? And if we do not know how to conduct ourselves properly, how can we educate our children to behave properly? It is imperative that we implement Aristotle's philosophy, the search for truth, before making any important decisions about how to live our lives. Only by having an understanding of the truth, or to word it another way, *the way things actually are*, can we determine how best to live. Only then are we in a position to educate our children properly.

It was my personal search for the truth and how I should conduct myself as a decent human being that led me to write this book. Before beginning my search, I first considered what I meant exactly by the truth. I recalled how there are, in fact, two types of truths which must be borne in mind. Philosophers sometimes refer to these as subjective truths and reasoned truths. Subjective truths are things which, for the foreseeable future at least, cannot be proved; things that are basically a matter of opinion. This includes questions such as 'Is there a God?', 'Is the universe infinite?' and so on. Reasoned truths are things which can be proved, things you can research and verify yourself – such as seven plus nine equals sixteen, or my height which is five feet ten inches.

Religion is a subjective truth. You either have faith that it is God's word telling you how to live, or you don't. Unfortunately this is unverifiable, and it may be that it is not God's word and you are not living your life the best possible way. It would be much safer and wiser if we based our conduct on things which are verifiable, tangible things which prove indisputably that we are better off behaving in a certain way.

Many people who are religious believe it is not possible to be a good person unless you subscribe exclusively to their faith. Religion and morals, for some, are inextricably linked; you should be good because God says you should be good. It is interesting that it is often the people who believe this the most strongly who are the ones that forget God's commandment '*Thou shalt not kill*': a philosophy many atheists never consider violating.

How to be Human uses reasoned truths, scientific facts that you can research and verify yourself (never blindly accept what anyone tells you). Using these, it explains why each and every one of us has a vested interest to be good regardless of whether we are religious or not.

Because this book addresses the fundamental way all humans should conduct themselves, if you are religious I think and hope you will find that the philosophies covered are in line with the core teachings of your faith.

How to be Human comprises the following four sections:

This is your time   An overview of creation from the big bang to you being here now.

Why be Good?   If you are not religious and if you do not believe in God, then why bother being good? Is there any universal truth we can derive from the universe to give guidance on the best way for humans to conduct themselves?

Why are we not Good? Explores why humans so frequently get it wrong by investigating positive, negative and destructive emotions plus moods, skewed perception, and extreme behaviour.

How to be Human By drawing on the previous sections a conclusion is reached on the best way for humans to conduct themselves. Having established this, some practical exercises show how we can meet this philosophy and increase our overall happiness, health and enjoyment of life as a result.

NB. Some subjective truths are included in the text in the form of philosophising unknowns, such as the nature of God. However the definitive reasons why we should be good are based on cutting edge scientific research.

Humans' biological make-up, our driving will to survive at all costs and hence put ourselves first, has led to the problems we see today in both interpersonal and intersociety relationships. But our social evolution is ongoing. It has led to now, a time when we are intelligent enough and wise enough to understand where and why we have got things wrong, and to set about starting to get things right. Humans love to segregate and label themselves, but history has shown where there is division there is conflict. We must break down all man-made barriers of race, religion, and politics. We must start, instead, from the standpoint that we are all human beings. The only division in society should be between those who understand the nature of their existence and live their lives in a peaceful harmonious way, and those who do not and suffer unhappiness as a result.

The Asian tsunami generated an unprecedented and extraordinary humanitarian response all over the world. Governments were led by the people and terrorist groups in some of the affected countries laid down their arms. A BBC news correspondent, when asked if he thought this coming together of the people would last, rather sombrely replied, "As time slips by, people do have a tendency to forget."

Well, I hope this book can go some way to ensuring that we do not forget. I hope it can help cultivate what was experienced in the world when the tsunami pushed the reset button, the barriers came down and, for a moment at least, we were reminded how to be human.

This
is your
time

Our Universe

How did you get here? How did you get here at this point in time, to be reading this book, right now? Before you say, 'Well, I just made a cup of tea, wandered through here, saw this book and…' I mean how did you, and everyone and everything else, get here? Trees, animals, the Earth, the planets, the sun, the stars, everything. Why is anything here? What's going on? Does it matter if you know or not? You have appeared in our world at this time, a living and breathing part of the most fantastic mystery. Like a character in a science fiction story you have woken up in a strange and curious land with no knowledge of what's gone before. Each new day is a chance for you to explore. It is a chance for you to seek out the truth, to try to find answers to why you are here and what's going on. But before you begin your adventure you must open your mind. You must prepare yourself to ask many questions. Only through application of an objective outlook will you stand any chance of unravelling the greatest

---

of mysteries, the mystery of how and why you, or any of us, are here now.

As children we quite naturally saw the magic in everything. Christmas Eve, fairytales and warm summer evenings made our eyes sparkle with excitement. If this joy in your existence has since faded, if your thoughts have become increasingly consumed with work and navigating life's obstacle course, then I am pleased to say there is an antidote. By equipping yourself with a basic understanding of our universe you will reignite the sense of awe, wonder and magic you experienced as a child. How you came to be here reading this book is more magical and enigmatic than any fairytale, and so incredible it would seem our belief as children, that anything is possible, may well be true after all.

Humans and everything in the universe are both individual and part of systems. These systems are, in turn, part of still bigger systems. Everything is interconnected and therefore everything that happens has an effect. Your behaviour has an effect. It has a negative or positive effect on your health, those around you and your environment. Jumping straight into life without giving any thought to your behaviour leads, at the very least, to upset. You will upset others and be upset by others. I believe the reason for this is because humans, like animals, are born essentially selfish and insular in nature. These are our default settings, if you like.

In order for us to maximise our health and happiness we must recognise our default settings and actively seek out the best way to behave. I do not believe we can truly know how to behave simply by passively doing as others tell us. After all, how do we know that what others tell us is true? To understand how best to conduct ourselves we must have some comprehension of the universe and how we came to be in it at this time. The only way we can obtain this is if we personally seek out the truth about our existence. So, as you can see, knowing something about how you came to be here reading this book now, and what's going on, most definitely does matter.

In this first section we will take a look at the universe of which you are a part. With this in mind, in the next section we will establish a Universal Truth (Natural Law) before developing the idea to show why, over and above anything else, it should be used as the basis for how humans conduct themselves. In the final section we will look at practical ways of implementing this philosophy and being healthier, happier, and living a more fulfilled life as a result.

So, are you ready to begin? Are you ready to begin the most incredible adventure, one to uncover the events which ultimately led to you being here now? If you are, then sit back and make yourself comfortable for this is going to be some journey. There is much that needed to happen to make your arrival on this planet possible.

On starting this chapter, and unbeknown to you, history slipped into reverse. Ever since, you have been accelerating back through time and have now reached a stage so far in the past that our universe is diminishing in size. Galaxies are drawing closer together and everything seems to be converging towards a single point. All light about you, indeed all light in our universe, is fading. By the time you finish reading this paragraph you will have travelled a staggering 14 billion years to within just a few moments of creation. Brace yourself, for you are about to arrive at the beginning...

The Big Bang!

It is 14 billion years ago. You see absolutely nothing. No Earth, no planets, no sun, no stars, and not a single atom; just utter, utter, blackness. Let the feeling of infinite nothingness engulf you for a few moments.

Suddenly, in the blackness, a tiny speck of brilliant white light appears. An instant later, it explodes. Pure energy spews out of the explosion and starts to spontaneously condense into elementary particles of matter. The elementary particles of matter combine to form atoms and the elements hydrogen and helium are born. The hydrogen and helium contract due to gravity and form large rotating clouds of gas. Regions within the rotating clouds condense still further and to such an extent that they heat up and form stars. Reactions take place inside stars to produce other elements such as carbon and oxygen. (Stars are element factories.) The older stars expand and explode, chucking all the elements they have made out into space (a supernova). The debris from these explosions coalesce into new stars, the heavier elements collecting together to form planets which orbit around them.

NB.   *This is an extremely simplified and condensed version of the big bang; the time between events in some instances is minuscule, and in others millions of years. (Stephen Hawking's 'The Universe in a Nutshell' provides a detailed chronology of events.)*

Our universe has been in a constant state of change since the big bang. It is expanding and cooling and new stars, planets, and galaxies are born whilst others die. Our star, the sun, formed from a cloud of rotating gas around 5 billion years ago. Earth formed from the same cloud around 4.6 billion years ago.

The following pictures are designed to give you an idea of the structure of our universe as it is today. The images represent what you would see if you were in a spaceship flying progressively further and further away from Earth. Imagine yourself in the spaceship looking out of the rear view window, watching everything retreat into the distance. Your journey ends looking back at our galaxy; just one of 200 billion galaxies in the universe (according to current estimates)!

NB. To minimise brain overload I have not included any distance measurements at all with the images. The distances and scales shown are so unimaginably massive as to be completely meaningless to most of us. (The 'Encyclopedia of Astronomy' provides detailed information on the size and scale of our universe.)

Drum roll please…

Structure of our Universe

1. Earth

Lift off!

2. Earth at a distance

Bye, bye...

3. Earth & Moon

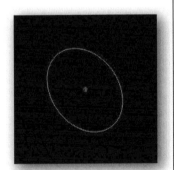

As you journey out into
space, you see the moon
orbiting the Earth.

4. Our Solar System

The Earth/Moon   The Sun
orbiting the Sun

Further out and you see
the Earth and other planets
orbiting the Sun.

5. Our Solar System starts to shrink

As you journey still further into space, our solar system appears smaller and smaller.

6. Our Solar System at a distance

Eventually our whole solar system shrinks to just a point of light. The stars nearest to us come into view (far right of diagram) and may have planets orbiting them just like in our solar system.

7. The Milky Way galaxy

Our solar system is in here.

Further out still you see our solar system is just one of billions that make up our galaxy. We call our galaxy, 'The Milky Way'.

8. Our Milky Way galaxy & local galaxies

Our Milky Way galaxy

Voyaging into the depths of space you see that our galaxy looks like a spiral disc. You also see neighbouring galaxies.

Do You Believe in God?

I magine the blackness just before the big bang. Suddenly from nowhere, a tiny speck of brilliant white light appears. From that light came the universe, everything you have seen on the preceding pages: Earth, the moon, the sun, and every star, planet, and galaxy. Absolutely everything, including life, is a manifestation of the energy flung from the big bang. Take a look at anyone or anything around you. You are looking at energy once a part of this divine light.

I completed writing this chapter in 2005. I wrote it from the perspective of an agnostic trying politely to explain what I, and indeed many others, believe to be the true nature of our universe. I thought that I had got everything sussed out. Philosophy and science have been a love of mine all my life and I have been what could probably best be described as an agnostic rationalist from around the age of 16. Consequently, for me, the universe and everything within it, was the subject of nature and natural processes; God was not required for everything to be the way that it is. Then in 2007 on Thursday, 2nd August at 7:27 p.m. my wife, Amanda, gave birth to our baby son, Samuel James Murray. Everything that unfolded in our lives since then has thrown my belief system up into the air and has led, some four years later, to me completely rewriting this chapter.

Samuel was the most incredible person I have ever had the privilege to spend time with. At the age of just one month old, family and friends commented that he seemed to be very knowing in his demeanour. 'Like an adult in a baby's body', many would say. We and others noticed wisdom about him, his beautiful, blue eyes emanating warmth and love. On taking him to baby groups it became apparent that he was blessed with the most wonderful social skills. Without any prompting, he quickly made himself the centre of group activities (frequently with children several years older), offering the other children raisins from the little box we had given him. Although only a baby, he displayed qualities that many do not attain in a lifetime: intelligence, charisma, kindness, emotional intelligence, and a tremendous sense of fun. He seemed quite naturally to be beautiful both inside and out. Amanda and I were incredulous that he had learnt this behaviour; it seemed to be innate. He was, at a most fundamental level, angelic in nature.

In September 2008, the unthinkable descended upon us. Samuel was diagnosed with a rare form of leukaemia. Immediately after his diagnosis he was admitted to Addenbrooke's Hospital, Cambridge, where he underwent an intensive six months of chemotherapy. Throughout the treatment, his incandescent personality remained intact.

He displayed great stoicism and strength, waving at nurses who had just performed horrendous procedures on him, and high-fiving Mummy and Daddy when suppressed fear leaked onto our faces. The consultants told us that the probability of Sam contracting this dreadful illness was around one in ten thousand. How could this happen to Sam? Why did it happen to us?

We lived at Addenbrooke's Hospital, more or less, for most of this six month period. As you can imagine the feeling that our world had been turned upside down was inescapable. Being disposed to thinking a lot about life occurrences, it is fair to say that I thought about the situation in which we now found ourselves from every conceivable angle, backwards and forwards. From the very beginning I experienced a conflict between my rational brain, which told me Samuel had been the victim of nature and pure bad luck, and my gut feeling, which was telling me something quite different.

As I said, I have been a secular and ardent rationalist for as long as I can remember. However, there were a couple of things which were beginning to shake my beliefs. (Unfortunately, it is difficult to say what these were without sounding like I am blowing my own trumpet - so please forgive me if it does!) The first of these was that if those among us who contract serious illnesses like leukaemia do so because of pure bad luck, as we were being told, then why had Samuel, such an unusually wise, intelligent, and beautiful child, fallen ill? Theoretically speaking, he should have been perfectly ordinary. The mathematicians among you will of course say, 'Well, given enough children who fall ill, some will inevitably be unusually wise and intelligent,' but this fails to explain the disproportionately high number of other children we met on Sam's ward who also seemed beyond their years.

Secondly, being with Sam and witnessing his suffering on a daily basis along with the suffering of all the other children on his ward and their families, was a practical lesson in the very qualities this book (which had already been written) aims to promote. I said many times that it felt as if I were being given a hands-on lesson in what I had been preaching. It occurred to me that the likelihood of a child contracting Sam's illness, and that child's father being the writer of a philosophy book designed to promote the very emotions he would subsequently experience daily, to be around one in a billion. (I assumed a figure of 1/100,000 for the number of people who would spend two years of their life writing a book like this.)

I must emphasise that these two thoughts did not make me think we, or the other families at the hospital, were being punished. On the contrary, they made me feel that these *special* children on Ward C2, and the dynamics of their families, were for some reason right for their collective experience.

Our beautiful son, Samuel James Murray, died at home on 2nd April 2009 at 1:26 a.m. aged just 20 months. As well as the horrendous sense of loss we felt losing Sam, we also experienced a second loss. During his six months of treatment we grew to convince ourselves (due largely to the thoughts just highlighted) that this was all happening for a reason, a spiritual learning exercise for our whole family which would culminate in Samuel's recovery and us all becoming better people. When he didn't make it, it felt like the plug was pulled on this idea.

Amanda and me had opened ourselves up to the possibility of there being a God but this door, as far as we were concerned, had now slammed firmly shut. We felt absolutely crushed having been through so much as a family. How could this whole business possibly be anything other than a random event? What good could come out of the death of such a beautiful little human being?

Surprisingly, these feelings only lasted for a couple of days up until a series of strange events which began the weekend after Samuel's passing. My brother and his wife came to stay with us and, taking advantage of the fact that they just happen to both be trained counsellors, we spent the entire weekend talking about Sam and everything that had happened.

On the Sunday, after a considerably late night spent in conversation, we wandered into town. After further lengthy discussion about life and our seemingly godless universe, my brother asked me a question which had the effect of clearing my mind of absolutely every thought: was it possible for me to sum up how I felt about the overall experience? For some reason, his question completely took me aback. I had literally nothing in my mind at all for what seemed like forever until, that is, the word *felt* began to filter through from my subconscious. I started to become aware in my mind's eye of a sense of whiteness, fading in somehow from the background to the foreground. In close accompaniment to this whiteness a feeling of love was beginning to emerge. Both whiteness and love grew brighter within me until utterly unmistakable. Suddenly I exclaimed, "I feel a sense of whiteness and love!" in answer to my brother's question and much to his, and my, surprise.

Shortly after this, we found out that both grandmas had experienced very curious dreams. Amanda's mum divulged that six months after Amanda fell pregnant she had had a dream in which she was looking after a baby, around a year old, that was listless and would not eat. She said that she was always fearful the dream would come true and even worried about Samuel getting leukaemia after he was born! A few days before his diagnosis, Sam had stayed with her for the night. By this stage, he was exhibiting exactly the behaviour that she had dreamed about. He was just over 13 months old. On telling my mum about this she said that she too had experienced a strange dream, but recently; only around three weeks before Samuel passed away. In her dream my mum said that she saw a small child standing on what seemed to be a swing. The swing gave the appearance of framing the child and the whole image was bathed in bright light. The child, who my mum said seemed neither a boy nor a girl, suddenly said, "I have done what I came here to do!" On waking, my mum was convinced that it was Samuel talking to her and she was fearful that he had passed away. She contacted us early at the hospital to see if everything was okay which, at the time and relatively speaking, it was.

Probably the strangest occurrence of all, though, happened to Amanda and me. From around the age of 10 months, Samuel developed a very funny habit of suddenly taking the dummy out of his mouth and chucking it some distance across the floor (with the distinct sense of an adult removing a jacket after a hard day's work and slinging it across the room!). Dummy chucking, it could be said, was a registered Samuel trademark.

One day after visiting Sam in the chapel of rest, we realised that he didn't have a dummy with him. We returned later that evening with his favourite yellow dummy and placed it next to him in the Moses basket. Amanda's sister and her husband had accompanied us and we were all walking back to the car together when, in the middle of me talking 19 to the dozen, I heard something fall to the ground and presumed that I had dropped something. I stopped and looked down to see what I had dropped. There at my feet was a yellow dummy, exactly the same type and colour as Sam's. I picked it up and stood staring at it, feeling confused.

"Didn't I just give this to Sam?" I asked Amanda.

Amanda too looked confused. On closer inspection we could see that, although it was exactly the same type and colour of dummy, it was slightly damaged and was not in fact Sam's, plus we confirmed with one another that we definitely had just left the dummy we had brought with us in Sam's Moses basket (something we double-checked the next day on visiting the chapel of rest). At this point, we both got the overwhelming feeling Samuel had performed one last dummy chuck, and in so doing was saying, "It's okay, Mummy and Daddy, I'm all right. This was meant to be!"

The important thing to stress here is that I truly believed the dummy fell from my pocket. I did not see it or kick it. I was only alerted to it by the clonk of something falling to the ground. Amanda and her brother-in-law later confirmed that they too had heard something fall to the ground and thought that I had dropped something.

It is impossible to convey the powerful feelings that experiences such as these induce unless you have had your own similar experiences. I was as sceptical as anyone about all things mystical until losing Sam and living and breathing the events which unfolded thereafter. During the course of caring for our son and losing him to leukaemia, I feel we got a glimpse of something much bigger, more beautiful, and more magical, than anyone could imagine. If you were to draw two lines on the ground one foot apart and say that this represented the sum total of human knowledge so far, it felt to me as if everything left to discover lay way beyond the second line, somewhere on the opposite side of the planet.

It occurred to me how many people, including me, cannot bear a failure to understand things. Clearly this quality is good in that it drives us to make new discoveries but, on the downside, it makes us prone to denying phenomena we have absolutely no understanding of. For many, I guess it is easier to say that something does not exist or is not possible rather than confessing to your ignorance on a subject.

Science frequently shows that the simplest explanation is the right explanation, and solutions to earthbound problems certainly seem to adhere to this. However, as far as our universe is concerned, this increasingly does not look the case. The deeper we probe into trying to understand our universe, the stranger and more mysterious have been our findings. For example, think back to the pictures of the universe shown on the preceding pages. It has been discovered that all of that lot, literally all the stars, planets, galaxies, absolutely everything we can *see*, only constitutes a mere 4% of our known universe! At present, an astonishing 96% of our universe remains invisible. (It is only detectable by its gravitational influence and we refer to it simply as dark matter and dark energy.) What exactly is going on in this 96%?

In addition to this, it is known that physics breaks down when you try to push further and further back towards the moment of the big bang (something physicists refer to as a singularity). Whether a relativistic or quantum mechanics approach is adopted, the mathematics always results in the same enigmatic answer: infinity. Physics has encountered a brick wall that scientists believe requires a genius like Einstein to get over.

There are other examples I could cite (our inability to reconcile relativity theory with quantum mechanics for example) but there is one gaping hole in our understanding which personally interests me over and above any other. Prior to losing Samuel I passionately believed, like most scientists, that consciousness was a product of the brain. So passionate am I about the subject of consciousness that originally 20% of this book was devoted to a chapter on it in which I denounced the independent existence of consciousness from the brain. Had it not been for our personal experiences, I believe I would never have changed from this viewpoint, but everything that has happened to us over the past year has led me to now rethink this belief.

I hope you get some measure of how powerful the effects of our experiences were by the fact that I decided to remove this entire chapter from the book (which was by far the longest to research and write and in many ways I was the most proud of). The dummy incident in particular led to this decision, but so too did the countless reports we subsequently read about other people's experiences. These, broadly speaking, can be summarised as follows:

- How do we explain out-of-body experiences in which people have accurately described events going on around them whilst medically unconscious?
- Why do people often report the same near-death experience (accelerating through a long tunnel towards a point of light, dissolving into light, merging with a greater light etc.)? Scientists tell us that when the body is under massive duress the brain releases endorphins to help relax us and calm us down, with hallucinatory effects similar to taking drugs. However, the hallucinations reported by drug users vary greatly, something which is not the case with near-death experiences. Some scientists argue that the experience is attributable to the way in which the brain shuts down, but it seems to me this is supposition. We know so little about the nature of consciousness that I believe we can't, at this stage, rule out anything.
- Why do people who recount near-death experiences often report conversations with spiritually enlightened beings which change their lives forever? Typically, the beings make clear that the material world is not what life is about and ask questions such as, 'What have you learnt about love?', 'What have you learnt about

compassion and kindness?' and, 'What knowledge and wisdom have you gained in your life?'

Prior to Samuel's passing, I was pretty obsessed with understanding in as much detail as possible how the universe came to be and why everything is the way that it is. I have grown to realise that there are, in fact, many, many unknowns, some of which we have only just begun to investigate (the phenomenon of consciousness, for example). No one person understands the whole picture and will not do so, at best, for some considerable time. I say 'at best' because it may be that we have to resign ourselves to never knowing how or why certain phenomena exist.

The German philosopher Immanuel Kant (1724-1804) believed that there are definite limits to what we can know, how far science and reason alone can get us.

He said (and I will paraphrase), "*The problem is that we are trying to understand a totality of which we ourselves are but a tiny part. We can never know, with certainty, this totality.*"

I now believe that there are no grounds on which to reject personal experiences sitting outside scientific explanation. Anyone who tries to dismiss your experiences is, at best, short sighted and, at worst, arrogant. Things deemed metaphysical today may well become scientific fact tomorrow. Other phenomena may remain enigmas and perhaps with good reason. Faced with so much uncertainty, I find myself increasingly enamoured by the philosophy of the Danish philosopher Soren Kieerkegaard (1813-1855) who said (paraphrased), "*Rather than searching for the ultimate truth of everything, it's more important to find the truth that's meaningful to the individual; 'the truth for me'. What matters is not whether your philosophy is true (for others), but whether it is true for you."*

Our personal experiences have opened my eyes to a wonderful, magical universe where, increasingly, anything appears possible. Not surprisingly, during the course of re-evaluating my beliefs I found myself asking, "Do I believe in God?" It occurred to me that despite how readily this question pops up throughout your life it is meaningless without first asking the following prerequisite question:

What do you, *personally*, perceive God to be?

I think many people still have a stereotypical perception of God as an old boy with a beard who created the universe. I say this because of the frequency with which you hear people ask, "How could God let this happen?" in response to different atrocities. (After Samuel passed away, I found myself asking Amanda, 'If there is a God, why did he let this happen?') But isn't it a tad naive to dismiss God on the grounds of this creator/guardian assumption? Isn't it just possible that God may be something altogether different? A question I now like to ask people is this:

Throughout history millions of people have reported strikingly similar spiritual experiences. With these, and all the unknowns about our existence in mind, can you be absolutely certain that there is no God, of any kind?

Currently, I find myself in a position where I still believe that the universe, and everything within it, is the subject of nature and natural processes. However, the spectrum of what I now deem to be natural is infinitely broader. I do not believe God created the universe, more like, God *is* the universe: a cyclic, beginning-less universe. I believe God is the energy that underpins all things (as opposed to a separate entity with the ability to intervene) and that a spiritual dimension exists. I also believe that each of us has our own spiritual objectives, a kind of life plan set out before we take on a physical form. I believe that Samuel, his family, our friends, and perhaps even you reading this now, were all meant to live through this experience so that we may spiritually evolve as a result. That being said, I passionately believe each of us has free will and can deviate from our life plans if we choose. I also passionately believe that we all have harmonious life plans and that God is in absolutely no way aggressive, vindictive, prejudiced, or an advocate of murder. For me, God is pure, selfless, unconditional love.

Of course I understand that these beliefs sound like utter nonsense to many people, and I have no problem with this. My beliefs are my beliefs, and your beliefs are yours; neither of us will ever be able to prove the other wrong. Our personalities, upbringing, culture, knowledge, and experiences forge how we think so we should be respectful of one another's views. The beliefs you personally hold, whether in a religious or secular context, are as valid as anybody else's provided, of course, that they do not cause harm to others.

It is unfortunate that, for many, religion is inextricably linked with God. It is unfortunate because for those with this belief, to distance yourself from religion means to distance yourself from God; something I firmly disbelieve. According to the gnostic gospels of *Didymos Judas Thomas* and *Mary Magdalene*, Jesus also disbelieved this. These two gospels portray Jesus as someone who believed that anyone can connect directly with God if they choose, and without a third party, church, or religion to do so. If this were Jesus's message, you can see how it got him into trouble. It is a radical idea now, let alone 2,000 years ago. It is radical because it makes God accessible to every human being on the planet, not just those who are religious. Furthermore, it is radical because it means religion is not required. All sentient beings are, by default, the children of God; indoctrination into human-born belief systems (potentially harbouring prejudice and hidden agendas) is unnecessary.

Of course, we will never be able to prove exactly what it was that Jesus believed but we can, nonetheless, think about the following question: if you were God, the most infinitely wise being in the universe, would you have a sign on your door saying, 'Christians only', 'Jews only', 'Muslims only', 'Hindus only', or 'Sikhs only'? In my view, God is not vain or jealous and does not discriminate. God, whatever you may perceive God to be, is directly available to each and every one of us who chooses to open our mind and heart.

'Sam's Story' by Amanda Murray details the life of our extraordinary son.

This is Your Time

Most people are accustomed to the idea of their family tree but few are aware that it can be traced back into an infinitely larger picture. You, me, every single plant, every single animal, and every single person that has ever lived are all part of one huge family tree, one extending back through evolution to the origins of life on our planet. If cameras had been around since the dawn of time, you may well have framed pictures of ape-like creatures hanging on your wall along with all the other family photos. And it does not stop there, for Earth too is part of its own family tree. The evolution of our universe has given rise to every single star, every single planet, and every single galaxy you can see in the night sky (and those you can't). Absolutely everything that exists, both life and the universe, can be traced back 13.8 billion years to a single speck of brilliant light and the start of creation.

It is incredible if you think of all the different boxes which needed to be ticked in order for you to exist now. Aside from the countless astronomical boxes needing to be ticked before life could even begin, and the path evolution needed to take for humans to evolve, consider how many people had to meet and procreate for you to eventually be born; any deviation whatsoever from this entire sequence of events may have resulted in someone different. Your family tree is in fact nothing less than the entire history of our universe! When you look at life in this way, you can see that each and every one of us is very privileged to exist at this time.

The path to each of us being here was a long and arduous one. I am glad most of us acknowledge this by celebrating our *birth* day, the moment we enter this physical realm. On Tuesday, 2nd December 1969 I was not in the world, but at 5:50 a.m. on Wednesday, 3rd December 1969, I was in the world; a thought which has always fascinated me.

Something else that has always fascinated me is recalling my earliest memory. Can you remember yours? Try to bring it to mind, your moment of incarnate awareness! My earliest memory is of my mum pushing me along in a red and black pushchair; me staring out at the world from behind a transparent screen, pulled down to keep the rain off my face. It was 1972, and I was just two years old at the time. Recently my mum and dad were tidying their loft and came across a baby book that they had made for me when I was born. Amongst all the typical information parents like to keep on their little ones, weight, size, how many Farley's Rusks I polished off in the course of a week and so on, I found a list of 'My First Visitors'. It was really weird seeing the names of people I later grew up to know, some of whom I still know to this day. Their lives were already well underway when I was born, then I came along and have been a part of their lives ever since. (Lucky them!)

Thinking about the world ticking along before we were born seems odd, almost as odd as thinking about it still ticking along quite happily when we are no longer here. But, of course, this has been the nature of human existence for millennia. Each generation is born, lives out their lives, and then makes way for the next generation to do exactly the same. Life, I think, is a little like the sun's reflection on the sea. Bright, twinkling lights appear for a while, dance around, and then disappear with the ebb and flow of each wave. As new lights appear, older ones disappear, with a gentle overlap between old and new. When looking at old photographs of people doing whatever it is they were doing, I like to speculate about their lives and what the world was like for them back then. I imagine walking into the photograph to say, "Hello, how's it going?" and wonder if I may have got on really well with someone who no longer exits. I expect the people of tomorrow might look at the pictures of today and wonder the same things.

So, the generations come and go and all that is left behind are some dusty, old photographs of times past. But just before I have you reaching for the tissues, I am very pleased to remind you that currently, *this is your time*. Our universe's continual evolution has resulted in you, me, and everyone we know, and everyone we don't yet know, existing at this moment in history. If you can appreciate the nature of your existence, and what it is you are a part of, you will be better equipped to live your life.

The philosopher Baruch Spinoza (1632-1677) believed we can only achieve true happiness and contentment if we understand how everything is related, everything is one; comprehending everything that exists in an all-embracing perception. He described this as seeing everything *sub specie aeternitatis* which, roughly translated, means:

'*To see everything from the perspective of eternity*'

Why be Good?

A Natural Law

> *"Let him who seeks continue seeking until*
> *he finds. When he finds, he will become*
> *troubled. When he becomes troubled, he will*
> *be astonished, and he will rule over the all."*

EXTRACT FROM THE *GOSPEL OF*
DIDYMOS JUDAS THOMAS.

To date, religion has probably been the main method for teaching how we should live wholesome and moral lives. You should be good because God says you should be good. But when you look at the conflict religion has caused and how morally speaking it seems to leave atheists out in the cold, one is forced to ask some rather sensitive questions. Has religion created more harm than good? Is it the only path to becoming a decent and moral person?

The German philosopher Immanuel Kant (1724–1804) believed, as do many today, that it is essential for human morality to believe in God. It is easy to see why when you consider the alternative. If you do not believe in God, if instead you believe there is no reason for our existence or anything that happens, a rather concerning question presents itself. Why be good? Why not do whatever you feel like doing? The belief that all morals and religions are irrelevant is known as nihilism and some despicable crimes have been carried out by nihilists who are often of high intelligence (Hitler, Stalin etc.). So, is religion and believing in God a necessity if we are to ensure people are moral and decent human beings? Are having these beliefs the only incentive for people to be good?

By the end of this section, we will have answers to these questions. They will be established during the process of answering an even bigger question and one that forms the basis for the rest of the book. This question is:

At the simplest level, what is the best way for human beings to conduct themselves?

Over the course of the following three sections, 'Why be Good?', 'Why are we not Good?', and 'How to be Human' we will concern ourselves with deriving a simple, coherent and reasoned answer to this and then detailing it in the last section, 'How to be Human'. The answer will be one based on verifiable, scientific fact. But where do we start? Is it actually possible to derive with reason alone a way in which humans should conduct themselves?

The Greek philosopher Socrates (470–399 BC) was concerned with finding universal truths for right and wrong, one could say a fundamental law that applies to all human beings. The Stoic school of philosophy (founded in Athens around 333-264 BC and influenced by Socrates) believed in a universal rightness embedded in nature itself, something they referred to as a *Natural Law*. Could it be possible that such a law exists? Is there anything we can derive from our universe to give guidance on how we should behave?

Our Harmonious Universe

The big bang gave birth to a universe in which all the forces of nature were in equilibrium. Every starting parameter was perfect, conducive from the offset to the formation of atoms. Once atoms had formed, the forces acting upon them ensured that increasingly complex atom systems emerged from the sea of particle chaos; first hydrogen and helium gases, then stars and planets. On the surface of at least one of these planets the most complex atom system to evolve so far came into being, DNA, and subsequently this led on to life.

All of these systems exhibit the most startling beauty. For instance, take a look at DNA molecules with their fantastic complexity and intricacy, or planets in orbit around a star. Every system, from the microcosm to the macrocosm, is graceful, beautiful, and harmonious. How can this be? Why is there so much harmony in a seemingly arbitrary universe?

Experience teaches us that harmonious systems outlive and outperform disharmonious systems but few people appreciate how significant this is. Harmony and balance permeate our entire universe on all conceivable levels. They govern the longevity and effectiveness of all systems whether atoms, stars, galaxies, organisms, families, work places, communities or football teams. If you take any system that has survived and performed well, you can deduce that it must be a harmonious system to have done so. You can deduce that it must be a system where the constituent parts act effectively together as an overall whole. To answer the question posed, the reason we see so much harmony in our universe is simple: disharmonious systems break down, whereas harmonious systems survive. Disharmony never outlives harmony and this is a fact of our universe.

Note for boffins: The second Law of Thermodynamics states that the total amount of disorder, or entropy, in the universe always increases with time. However, the law refers only to the total amount of disorder. The order in individual bodies can increase, provided that the amount of disorder in their surroundings increases by a greater amount. This chapter and book is primarily concerned with the longevity of systems after they have come into existence.

Living systems are an excellent example of how harmony and balance shape absolutely everything. Successful organisms like humans (and some animals) exhibit harmony on at least three levels, which I personally refer to as Physical Harmony, Evolutionary Harmony, and Social Harmony.

Physical Harmony is how I like to refer to the unbelievable amount of harmony in our human construction. To illustrate just how physically harmonious we are, imagine the difficulty in building a machine to perform as well as a human at all the different tasks a human can perform. Imagine how difficult it would be, for instance, to build a machine that could beat a human at tennis. We, like many animals, have the ability to flow smoothly and quickly from one movement to the next, we are dynamic and can react to change in any situation, rather than being restricted to preset, machine-like behaviour. It is because our brains and bodies are so harmonious that we are such diverse and effective systems.

Evolutionary Harmony is the term I use for the harmony that exists between an organism and its environment, and between one species and another. The process of evolution has created harmony in nature through a continual refinement of life. Organisms not well suited to their environment die out, whilst organisms better suited survive. In this way the environment acts like a kind of filter, ensuring only organisms that are harmonious with it remain in the world. The survivors undergo an ongoing process of fine tuning by the environment and climate in which they live. Physical attributes conducive to survival prevail (stronger limbs to chase prey etc.) and are passed on to future generations. Species gradually become better equipped for survival. But as well as the harmony between organism and environment gradually increasing, the harmony that exists between different species also increases. Predators that hunt smaller animals will evolve teeth more suited to eating meat i.e. the predator evolves with its prey in mind. In a similar way, the hunted animals may evolve hard shells or bristles to help protect themselves i.e. the prey evolves with its predator in mind. In this way, species become interdependent on each other. Organisms are designed to rely on other organisms and their environment for survival, a sudden change in either of these things potentially leading to extinction.

Social Harmony is how I refer to the harmony exhibited within some species to improve the chance of survival, both of the individual and the species as a whole. For example, individually ants are not very bright, but working as a team they build complex nests and communities; as do bees, termites and many other creatures. By working collectively, each member of the community adds to the overall strength, capabilities and sophistication of the group.

Humans are a species that evolved exactly in this way, to be interdependent on one another in a changing environment. To illustrate this, consider how many people are involved in keeping your life running smoothly. If you think about this carefully, you should realise just how dependent you and everyone else is on other people. We depend on others to build and repair our houses, to supply us with water and energy, grow our food, make our clothes, keep our streets tidy, take care of us when we are ill, entertain us, and so on. It would be impossible for each of us to do all these different jobs ourselves, yet all are necessary for our standard of living to be as sophisticated as it is. Only by working collectively as a team can we accomplish the vast array of jobs required to maintain our advanced human society.

You may think we work solely to get money to enjoy our lives, but this is only part of the story. For what is money, exactly? Have you ever wondered how our species got to the stage where we are so preoccupied with rectangular pieces of paper and round metal discs? Money is a human construct. It is a method we have devised to ensure all parts of our team remain functional, both for the survival of each team member and the team as a whole. It is merely a catalyst driving humans to work collectively so that we may all enjoy a better life as a result. Ultimately, we are no different from bees, ants and termites, working together for the good of each member of the community. Money is simply our human way of achieving this.

So, harmony and balance not only shape the entire structure of the universe, from DNA to stars and galaxies, they also regulate the organisms that inhabit it and on all conceivable levels. The fate of absolutely everything in existence, whether animate or inanimate, depends on how stable, balanced, and harmonious it is. If we draw inspiration from the philosophy of the Stoics, we could describe this fact as a Natural Law of our universe and summarise it as follows:

Natural Law: Harmonious systems survive and perform well; disharmonious systems do not.

This Natural Law could be thought to have been born the moment our universe was created. It is something inherent within everything that has ever existed and everything that will ever exist, a consequence of individual elements combining to form a larger system. But interesting as this may be, it is somewhat vague in terms of how humans should conduct themselves. Is there nothing more concrete we can say on this matter?

The next chapter aims to build upon the Natural Law and move closer towards an answer to our question, *'At the simplest level, what is the best way for human beings to conduct themselves?'* It attempts to do this by investigating what, on the surface at least, seems to be an unrelated subject…

Happiness

If you embrace the gift of life, I believe you *automatically* embrace the desire to be happy. I believe the desire to be happy is a natural and mandatory part of living, not an optional extra. For instance, if someone were to try to argue (albeit bizarrely) that they like being unhappy, they would effectively be saying that unhappiness brings them a perverse degree of happiness, in which case happiness would still be their objective. Individuals may or may not be happy at different stages in their life, but everyone desires to be as happy as possible, for as much of their lives as possible.

To most of us this is patently obvious but there are some who, whilst lucky enough to be living in peaceful countries, treat happiness as if it were a sin, as if there were an 11th commandment, *'Thou shalt not be happy'*. Over the years I have worked with a few people who played down good news, who avoided showing excitement at anything. The only reason I can attribute to this is a belief that to openly express positive emotion is uncool, whereas to openly express negative emotion (particularly cynicism and anger) is cool. But happiness is neither a sin nor something to be considered uncool and hopefully this chapter will show why such beliefs are foolish. Furthermore, happiness is not a luxury reserved for the wealthy (surveys show wealthy people are generally no happier than anybody else) or any other elite group. Once the basic necessities are taken care of e.g. we have shelter, a healthy diet, are getting enough sleep, are getting enough exercise, have reasonably good physical and mental health, and live somewhere with relative social stability, it is something attainable by us all. Happiness is each and every human being's fundamental right.

Before continuing, it is important that I differentiate between short-term happiness (pleasure) and true, lasting, long-term happiness (our day-to-day feeling of happiness). Most people experience the former on and off throughout their lives but much fewer experience the latter. Short-term happiness is subjective and can be obtained easily from numerous different sources. Some people get a fix of happiness when buying new clothes, eating out or going on holiday, whilst others require more extreme stimuli, such as promiscuous sex, drugs, or even violent crime. Whatever the source, the happiness induced is short-lived, lasting for the duration of the stimulus only, or fading soon after. Long-term happiness is not so easily found. It is not something which can be bought but does have the advantage of being within everyone's grasp, reliant on nothing more than oneself.

This chapter focuses on how each of us can improve our lasting, long-term happiness and avoid the need for an endless supply of happiness fixes. You may think this a self-indulgent exercise and, if so, I am pleased to say that you are wrong. Scientific surveys consistently show that happy people are more beneficial to society; more sociable, altruistic, loving, forgiving, proactive, optimistic and performing better in whatever they do. Conversely, surveys also show that unhappy people are less beneficial to society; more antisocial, self-centred, argumentative, non-proactive, pessimistic, cynical and performing worse in whatever they do. So, it is not only individuals who benefit from being happier, the society of which they are a part also benefits. But whilst this is all well and good, isn't long-term happiness solely dependent on nature, a day-to-day happyometer wired into our brains at birth?

Scientific research indicates that this is not the case. By the end of this chapter you will see that each of us has the potential to improve the default happiness setting nature gave us. In the final chapter of the book, 'Spirituality', we look at two different ways in which this can be done, both of which have proven effective when practised regularly. But until then, let us begin our quest for lasting happiness with a question; a question that is fundamentally important and yet many people never ask. Think about the following carefully, before answering honestly:

On an average day, all things considered, how happy do you feel on a scale of one to ten?

I believe the reason people do not ask this question (or choose to answer it dishonestly) is for fear of the truth. For instance, consider an executive who, on the surface, has everything: a high salary, large house, expensive car, nice family, regular holidays abroad etc. but who nonetheless, when honest, awards herself a low score. Assuming she has worked very hard for these things, a low score would clearly undermine her world. She would be compelled to ask herself, 'What was it that drove me to work for everything I have?'

Western culture leads us to believe such acquisitions are the path to happiness, but this is misleading. I say misleading because I do not want to suggest that it is wrong to work hard for a nice house (like all animals, we enjoy our creature comforts!) but merely point out material things in themselves do little to improve our long-term happiness. If we have food to eat and a warm and stable environment, this is pretty much all we need. Cars, DVD players and satellite TV are all very much short-term fixes of happiness. Once we have grown used to them, we settle back down to our default happiness setting. And whilst we should feel proud of our achievements, we should not succumb to the delusion that *material superiority = happiness*. Some people believe that because they own a big house or an expensive car they must be happier than those who do not, they like to remind other people of their superior material status. But, of course, this type of behaviour simply results in them losing friends and damaging their own long-term happiness. No-one enjoys being used to make others feel happier. (Incidentally, never try to keep up with the Joneses; remind yourself instead that they are deluded and that material superiority does not equal happiness.) So, where can we look to increase our default happiness setting, our personal on board regulator of lasting happiness?

There is a famous story of the Greek philosopher Diogenes (412-323 BC) who reputedly lived in a barrel and owned nothing but a cloak, a stick, and a bread bag. It is said that one day, while Diogenes was sitting beside his barrel enjoying the sun, he was visited by Alexander the Great. The emperor stood before him and asked if there was anything he could do for him, was there anything he desired? 'Yes,' Diogenes replied, 'could you stand to one side please, you're blocking the sun.'

The Foundations for Lasting Happiness

I believe it was Albert Einstein who once said, "Most people are consumed by the trivialities of living." If it was, I assume he did not mean by this that we should all sit down and write *'On The Electrodynamics of Moving Bodies'*, but instead was trying to draw our attention to the superficial existence many people lead. If life for you seems solely to consist of getting up, going to work, eating, then going back to bed before starting the whole process over again, you are likely to experience a midlife crisis around 35-45 years old. You will feel, understandably, that life is hollow, that it has no meaning. You will crave happiness fixes aplenty.

The first step toward achieving true, lasting, long-term happiness is to realise what a narrow perception of reality this is. We do not exist independently of everyone and everything; we are a part of everyone and everything. We are a part of the vast interconnected system we call our universe. As you move through the picture, so to speak, it changes around you. History is continually being made and you play your part in making it. Life only has context when your perception of reality is the overall picture of which you are a part. When it is and you understand something about being in it at this time, your wonder and appreciation of life greatly increases. Your day-to-day happyometer reading nudges up a level. Proactively cultivating your gratitude, forgiveness, optimism and ability to see the good in things will help to nudge it up another couple of levels, but I am pleased to say this is only the beginning. The rest of this chapter shows the potential we all have to increase our happyometer reading still further.

Universal Morals

Socrates believed that it is not possible to be truly happy if we know deep down what we do is wrong. If you think about this for a few moments, you should see what an optimistic philosophy this is. It is optimistic because, if true, means that by simply modifying our behaviour we can improve our day-to-day feeling of happiness. However, there is one thing we will need to address before we can place ourselves in the long-term happiness driving seat. What exactly constitutes right and wrong conduct (good and bad behaviour)?

Unlike Socrates, some philosophers believed that right and wrong conduct or morals vary from generation to generation and also from culture to culture (the branch of philosophy dealing with morals, 'ethics', is a derivative of a Greek word meaning *custom*). The ideal would be for morals to be based on, or derived from, something that transcends generation and culture. Such *universal morals* could then be used to guide human behaviour in the direction of good conduct and in so doing, if Socrates is correct, improve our long-term happiness. But what source could we use to derive these happiness-inducing morals from?

Like all other organisms, humans' top biological priority is survival and reproduction. When our chance of survival is good, nature rewards us with an increased feeling of happiness. When our chance of survival is not so good, nature warns us with a decreased feeling of happiness. In serious situations where our life is in danger we experience fear, a powerful emotion galvanising us to take immediate evasive action and one diametrically opposed to happiness. Our will to survive, and the emotions we experience to ensure that we do, are universal. They are not something dependent on generation, culture or matter of opinion, but are a biological fact.

How well we are surviving is the most significant factor in determining our happiness, and, because of this, forms a logical base from which we can derive these two morals:

Any behaviour which increases our   = *Good*
chance of survival (and consequently increases
our prospect of long-term happiness)

Any behaviour which decreases our   = *Bad*
chance of survival (and consequently decreases
our prospect of long-term happiness)

If you live in a peaceful and affluent country like Britain you are lucky in that probably the greatest threat to your survival is a loss of health; looking after yourself is a prerequisite for happiness. That being said, could we perhaps develop these essentially generic morals into something a little more usable?

In the previous chapter we drew inspiration from the Stoics and established our own Natural Law which we defined as follows:

Natural Law: Harmonious systems survive and perform well; disharmonious systems do not.

This law summarises how the fate of absolutely everything in existence, whether animate or inanimate, is dictated by how stable, balanced, and harmonious it is. And of course this goes for humans too. People who are harmonious and balanced in themselves, with those around them and with their environment should theoretically have a longer, more harmonious life.

Our generic morals state that any behaviour which increases our chance of survival is good. Therefore, the Natural Law can be used to refine them into more universal morals as follows:

Universal Morals:

Harmonious Behaviour = Good
(Increases our chance of survival, how well we perform &
our long-term happiness)

Disharmonious Behaviour = Bad
(Decreases our chance of survival, how well we perform &
our long-term happiness)

These basic morals are, I believe, unaffected by generation, culture and other transient factors. But how exactly can we use them to help us achieve lasting happiness?

Achieving Lasting Happiness

In '*The Art of Happiness*', the Dalai Lama says, "*I believe that the very purpose of our life is to seek happiness.*" The book explains that the path to happiness is made easier by an underlying sense of moving toward happiness in all that we do, by framing the decisions we have to make each day with the question (paraphrased): 'Will this improve my *long-term* happiness?' For instance, imagine someone tempted by the prospect of a wild and torrid affair; an intense, but temporary, happiness fix. If the individual considers his long-term happiness, he will see that guilt, divorce, and a lifetime of regret are poised to ruin it, that as with drugs, the long-term 'down' of an affair far overshadows the short-term 'high'. Only by considering his long-term happiness can a lifetime of regret be avoided.

Unfortunately many decisions we must make each day are not clear cut. Frequently it is not at all obvious what is the right or wrong thing to do or which choice, if any, has the potential to increase our long-term happiness. I believe that the concept of Universal Morals can be employed to help us see situations more clearly. To see how, let us first combine them with our happyometer idea to form one mental image:

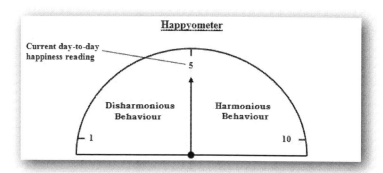

When faced with the difficulty of deciding on a correct course of behaviour, bring this aide-mémoire to mind. Envisage harmonious behaviour increasing your long-term (day-to-day) happiness reading, and disharmonious behaviour decreasing it. *Harmonious behaviour* can be characterised as behaviour which is selfless and may/does improve the well-being of others. *Disharmonious behaviour* can be characterised as behaviour which is selfish and may/does worsen the well-being of others. If you navigate through life with the intention of increasing your harmonious behaviour and diminishing your disharmonious behaviour, your happyometer reading will steadily climb.

NB1 *If you engage in a harmonious act which results in no effect on the well-being of others, or worse, accidentally worsens the well-being of others, this does not nullify the harmonious act. Similarly, if you engage in a disharmonious act such as having an affair but to date have not been found out, this does not nullify the disharmonious act. In my view, harmonious* *(moral) acts and disharmonious (immoral) acts are indepen-dent of outcome, hence the use of 'may/does' in the definition above. Unfortunately the outcome of an act may reduce the respective rise or fall of your happyometer reading.*

NB2 *Many day-to-day acts, for example making a cup of tea, are neutral or functional. That is, they are neither harmoni-ous nor disharmonious. They may increase your immediate short-term happiness but will have little or no effect on your long-term happiness.*

NB3 *Invariably, selfless acts are required at the most inopportune moments! Be mindful of this and be ready to make others your top priority when suddenly your help is needed.*

The following are two everyday examples of where the Universal Morals can be employed:

Conversational Harmony

Surveys show that people who get on well with others and have a good social life are generally healthier and happier. Humans, like many other mammals, are gregarious in nature. We flour-ish when part of a group, when we feel that we are well liked. Anything we can do to improve our social life will ultimately improve our happiness, so how we converse is crucial.

Conversations are probably the easiest time to practise be-ing a harmonious individual. Many people give little thought to what they say to others or the effect that their conversation has. Yet each of us has our own personal history, hopes and fears, strengths and weaknesses. We should try to be considerate of this when talking; conscious of affecting people in a positive or negative way and prepared to adjust or temper our conversation if necessary. If we do not, if instead we are consumed solely with what we want to say, it is only a matter of time before we upset someone. When conversational harmony breaks down, future encounters may be frosty or hostile, the friendship or associated friendships perhaps disbanding. Whichever it is, being disharmonious towards others always results in the same thing: a reduction of *our own* happyometer reading.

Difficult People

Difficult people may seem to be an exception to this rule. If someone is disharmonious towards you, surely you can reciprocate? Well, as far as your long-term happiness is concerned this is a fallacy. Consider somebody you have known who was rude or obnoxious. How did you deal with them? Perhaps you were rude back to them or perhaps you chose to walk away, stewing on the things that they had said or done. If this is how you dealt with the situation then how did your response make you feel? Happier or less happy about what had happened? When you bear in mind that difficult people are actually venting their unhappiness, in a way we should feel sorry for them. It is difficult, but imagine instead how you would have felt if you had responded to this person in a selfless harmonious way, if you had responded firmly, but also with pity and love?

The Dalai Lama says that the best way to deal with trying situations is to see them as an opportunity to better yourself. Use them to practise increasing your patience, tolerance and self-control; all qualities which, as it turns out, help to increase your happyometer reading. He says we should consider such situations a challenge; a challenge to combat our anger, impatience and intolerance which are destructive emotions that rob us of our happiness. (He describes anger as our true enemy.) And remind yourself too that exposure to the bad in the world helps you better appreciate the good.

These small examples of how the concept of Universal Morals can be employed to help us pick the right course of behaviour, and in turn increase our happyometer reading, is of course just the tip of the iceberg. There is much disharmonious behaviour that is infinitely worse than falling out with people (physical abuse, rape, murder etc.). Personally, I believe that the more severe someone's behaviour is, the greater the swing in their happyometer reading:

> *Very good (harmonious) behaviour = large positive swing*

> *Very bad (disharmonious) behaviour = large negative swing*

But is there any evidence which actually backs up this idea that there is a link between our behaviour and our happiness?

Are Behaviour and Happiness Linked?

Richard J Davidson (Professor of Psychology and Psychiatry at the University of Wisconsin-Madison) conducted experiments which revealed that when people have high levels of brain activity in a region within the left prefrontal cortex part of the brain, they report feelings such as happiness, enthusiasm, high energy and alertness. Conversely, he found that when people have high levels of brain activity in a region within the right prefrontal cortex part of the brain, they report feelings such as sadness, anxiety, and worry. Each of us has a characteristic ratio of left-to-right activation that is a direct indication of the moods we are likely to feel each day. Science has shown that our brains really do possess happyometers!

When Davidson and others looked at this ratio in Buddhist monks, they made an exciting discovery. The monks showed a much higher ratio than anybody else tested at that point i.e. their day-to-day feelings of happiness were significantly higher than anybody else's. To understand why, further experiments were carried out and the following conclusion was reached: *People who exhibit predominantly harmonious qualities, such as love, compassion, kindness and empathy, experience high levels of lasting happiness, but people who exhibit predominantly disharmonious qualities, such as anger, fear, jealousy and desire (or derivatives such as irritability, anxiety, greed and aversion), experience low levels of happiness.*

In addition to this, Davidson and his team made two other exciting discoveries. The first was that the left-to-right ratio we all have is not fixed. Instead, we can improve our ratio (our happyometer reading) by increasing our harmonious qualities and decreasing our disharmonious qualities. The second finding was that in doing this we not only increase are day-to-day feeling of happiness, we also increase the effectiveness of our immune system. Put simply, the happier you are, the healthier you are!

The science can be summarised as follows:

Harmonious Qualities => *Increase feeling of happiness + Strengthen immune system*

Disharmonious Qualities => *Decrease feeling of happiness + Weaken immune system*

Scientists are now in agreement with Buddhists. We can increase our happiness by cultivating harmonious emotions, thoughts and behaviour and reducing, or ideally eliminating, disharmonious emotions, thoughts and behaviour. But how exactly can we go about this?

Cognitive Behavioural Therapy (CBT) is an effective technique used by psychiatrists for treating sufferers of anxiety, depression and OCD. It is based around the discovery that we can change the wiring in our brain (and hence our thoughts and emotions) by changing our behaviour. A phrase sometimes administered to patients is, *'change your behaviour and your thoughts will follow'*. CBT demonstrates that there is a link between behaviour and thought, that one mirrors the other.

This means that if we adopt more harmonious behaviour, we change the wiring in our brain and develop more harmonious thoughts and emotions. This in turn increases our happiness. Alternatively, if we adopt more disharmonious behaviour, we develop more disharmonious thoughts and emotions and this will decrease our happiness.

Therefore, behaviour and happiness are indeed linked and their relationship can be expressed as follows:

Behaviour <=> Thoughts & Emotions => Happiness & Health

The two-way arrow between Behaviour and Thoughts & Emotions indicates that changing one side of the equation will change the other.

Meditation has been found to be another technique that can be used to change the wiring in the brain. It makes possible the direct cultivation of harmonious emotions such as compassion, which in turn increase harmonious behaviour and happiness. We will look at both CBT and meditation in the final chapter, 'Spirituality'.

Happiness Conclusion

You may have heard people say that happiness comes from within, that it is determined by your state of mind. Indeed, all historical studies up to and including the latest scientific research point to this being the case. Lasting happiness cannot be found by buying a new car or a big house, and it cannot be found by taking drugs or beating someone up. These are fallacies which stem from neither understanding what happiness is nor how to attain it. True and lasting happiness is the emotional state we experience *only* when our mind is calm, balanced, and harmonious; nature's way of telling us that we are optimised for survival. Like all living things, survival is our top priority. I believe that happiness is a measure of how well we are faring.

Thoughts and emotions are instrumental in our behaviour; change one side of the equation and you will change the other. Science has shown that disharmonious thoughts and emotions are detrimental to your health and happiness. For example, people prone to cynical distrust have been found to be at a higher risk of hardening of the arteries, whilst a wealth of evidence shows that anger, hatred and hostility are as damaging to the cardiovascular system as high cholesterol and high blood pressure. It is possible that these severe, destructive emotions may be even worse! By contrast, science has shown that when we cultivate harmonious thoughts and emotions (and in particular when we cultivate love and compassion), we increase our happiness, improve our health, and are better at rapidly recognising emotions in others. Buddhists say there are also other benefits of cultivating compassion. Things they mention include being loved by people and animals, having a serene mind, sleeping and waking peacefully, and having pleasant dreams.

The conclusion of this chapter and section can be summarised as follows:

*If we cultivate the harmonious qualities inherent within us, **love**, **compassion**, **kindness** and **empathy**, we will increase our day-to-day feeling of happiness and have better health.*

*If we succumb to the disharmonious qualities inherent within us, **anger**, **fear**, **jealousy** and **desire** (or derivatives such as **irritability**, **anxiety**, **greed** and **aversion**), we will decrease our day-to-day feeling of happiness and damage our health.*

The Gospels of Thomas and Mary imply that Jesus taught a similar, Buddhist-like philosophy.

All humans desire health, happiness and a long life. To maximise these things we must be harmonious or to put it another way, we must be good. Therefore, all humans have an incentive to be good. This is the case regardless of whether you are religious or believe in God.

The objective of *How to be Human* is to answer the question, 'At the simplest level, what is the best way for human beings to conduct themselves?' The logical answer derived so far is:

To be happy, be good.

Why are we not Good?

Emotions

One evening in January 2006, a Londoner, aged 31, was murdered on his way home from work. Two youths followed him out of a tube station, kicked him from behind and stabbed him in the leg when he tried to fight them off. They chased him down the street where he lived and caught up with him then stabbed him in the arm, face and twice in the chest as he tried to defend himself. The assailants left the man to die in the gutter. His wedding plans were strewn over the pavement while his fiancée waited at home for his return. The youths were convicted of murder but showed no remorse for their crime. The price they put on a human being's life: just £20 and a mobile phone.

On hearing horrendous stories like this, most of us ask the same questions, 'What is it that drives people to commit such monstrous crimes?' and 'How can anyone be so callous, wicked and cruel?' This chapter aims to unravel the root causes of disharmonious behaviour and culminates with a breakdown of factors which, I believe, contribute to the most extreme cases.

Emotions evolved in humans and animals in order to increase their chance of survival. They affect physiology (heart rate, breathing etc.) and generate a strong desire to engage in a particular course of behaviour. Situations and thoughts generate emotions. The intensity of the situation or thought affects the intensity of the emotion experienced. For example, something may mildly irritate you or instead make you very angry. Emotions are very important because they both instigate our behaviour and determine the level to which we engage in that behaviour. Love and compassion, for instance, ensure that mothers bond with their infants. Fear and anger, on the other hand, ensure we are equipped with a fight-or-flight response to dangerous situations. And happiness, I believe, gauges how well we are faring, both physically and mentally; it encourages us to engage in certain behaviour only.

Emotions evolved in animals millions of years before any of them could reason (strategies to catch prey etc.). The thinking brain, or neocortex, evolved from the emotional areas; there was an emotional brain long before there was a rational one. A consequence of this is that we may sometimes feel an emotion before we have time to compute what is going on. In very intense or rapidly changing situations, we may launch into action and only later realise why we did so. Animals with little or no ability to reason are always in this boat. They are bound by their emotions and are forced to react in accordance with them when they arise.

Humans are endowed with more control. Emergency situations aside, we have the capacity to monitor our emotions, to intercept the impulse to act and ask, 'Hold on a minute, is this the best thing to do?' How adept we are at this is referred to as *Emotional Intelligence*. It has been found that people who excel in all walks of life have struck a harmonious balance between their emotional response to situations (which occurs very quickly) and their rational response; they are experts at both managing their emotions and recognising emotions in others.

Moods

Unlike emotions, which can come and go in a matter of seconds or minutes, a mood is a kind of drawn-out emotion. It is a sustained emotional feeling which can last all day and may have no obvious cause. When the origin of a mood is unknown, it is believed that it may be down to chemical changes within us; things such as alcohol, drugs and a lack of food or sleep are all known triggers. A good example of this type of mood is waking up on the wrong side of the bed; a cup-of-tea followed by some fresh air will hopefully restore the balance. Other known causes of depressed moods include things like a loss of health or fitness, an oppressive environment, bad weather or a personal loss. Known causes of happy moods include good health & fitness, a harmonious environment, sunny weather, personal accomplishments (no matter how small compared to other people) and the feeling of acquiring knowledge. The chemical balance of young children is particularly sensitive. Too much sugar, combined with too little sleep and insufficient exercise, can cause dramatic temper tantrums. For persistent moods, with no apparent cause, specialist treatment may be required (for example counselling, psychoanalysis or medication).

Perhaps the most common cause of moods is prolonged exposure to an emotion. When we experience a succession of pleasant events (and therefore pleasant emotions) it generally induces a happy mood, but several frustrating or upsetting events in succession will cause our happiness level to dip. Obviously some things during the course of the day are outside our control, but one thing which is not is how we choose to conduct ourselves. We saw in the previous chapter how harmonious behaviour increases our happyometer reading and disharmonious behaviour decreases it. We mentioned too how some people believe that it's cool to be downbeat and cynical (a trend perhaps initiated by film and rock stars). If you regularly choose to be mean and moody, the reality is that you will rewire your brain and eventually end up feeling mean and moody. We become the person we act being (a more severe example follows at the end of this chapter). To attain a prevailing happy mood, you must therefore not only conduct yourself harmoniously, you must also adopt a prevailing harmonious and happy manner.

Destructive Emotions

Emotions could be categorised as harmonious or disharmonious but usually they are referred to as positive (constructive) or negative. Positive emotions, such as compassion, love and happiness, lead to harmonious behaviour. They are beneficial to you and to others. Negative emotions, such as anger, fear, jealousy and desire, lead to disharmonious behaviour that is often harmful to you and to others. I say often because anger and fear evolved for a reason. These powerful emotions are vital in life-threatening situations, for instance if we, or our children, are under attack. But when experienced in other far less threatening situations, as is much more often the case, they are harmful. The definition of a *destructive emotion*, as used in this chapter, can be summarised as follows:

> *A destructive emotion is a negative emotional response to a situation which does not require it.*

Children are sometimes naughty because of social ignorance; that is, they have not yet learned how to conduct themselves. On other occasions, and in the case of adults, destructive emotions often underpin disharmonious/destructive behaviour. They are frequently the root cause of why people are not good, whether it is someone who is mildly rude or a vicious and ruthless dictator. If we can understand their cause and how to deal with them, we can set about tackling the distress and misery they unleash.

What Causes Destructive Emotions?

Certain genetic and biological conditions are known to disrupt brain wiring in infants and result in a destructive predisposition.

Head injuries, drugs, and alcohol can all increase destructive emotions, either temporarily (as many of us have experienced) or permanently (as in cases of severe head injury and drug/alcohol addiction). So too can repetitive bad behaviour. If you change your actions, your thoughts and emotions will follow. Probably the biggest cause of destructive emotions though is what I would call mental knocks and bumps; an accumulation of mental scars caused by our life experiences, particularly bad emotional experiences.

I once saw a beautiful analogy of this which likened a child's mind to a clear glass of water. As the child grows, the water becomes gradually muddied by life's upsets, while beneath all the impurities clear water remains. An example with which many of us are familiar is the grumpy old man, someone who gets increasingly jaded and cynical with age, not the happy-go-lucky person we once knew. In the final chapter, 'Spirituality', we will look at how to remove these impurities from our minds. But first, let us look at three simple examples which demonstrate how the destructive emotions hate, fear and jealousy could develop:

Hate: The Big-Nosed Yobs

Imagine that, when you were young, you were seriously beaten up by a gang of big-nosed yobs. You were frightened for your life and, after a stay in hospital, ended up with permanent facial scars which you felt people were always looking at and which you believed hampered your relationships with others. Imagine now that at some future date you have dealings with someone who has a big nose. Every time you look at this person, the memories come flooding back. You are reminded of the fear you felt that night and your fear soon turns to anger. You feel angry because, as you see it, those big-nosed yobs ruined your relationships with others. If it wasn't for them, everything would be okay. People with big noses are bad news and the world would be a much better place without them. (Humans have a tendency to stereotype, to tar groups of people with the same brush.) Eventually, these feelings become too much. You get into a ridiculous argument with your associate and before you know it you've punched him…on the nose.

Fear: The Sausage Roll Disaster

Attending a birthday party when I was a child, I got into a sausage roll eating competition (as you do) with my friend Scotty. Needless to say, what with the chocolate fingers and lashings of lemonade consumed earlier, I suddenly found myself vomiting rather spectacularly over the living room carpet, bringing a rather abrupt end to our game of Pass the Parcel. The event was infinitely more embarrassing than I could have imagined. My mum was called to pick me up early and I was led away disgraced; head bowed, no doubt just visible above the living room window I mooched past on my way home. For the next few years, I was left with a fear of eating in front of people in case I vomited again. I made excuses when invited to subsequent parties, but on occasions when I couldn't get out of it, family get-togethers and so on, I felt terrified on smelling that egg and cress sandwich, chocolate finger smell. I remember getting hot on the back of my neck, and feeling like I was going to faint.

Jealousy: Sociable Susie

Imagine that you were a shy child who had struggled to make friends. You were regularly upset about being the outsider and feeling lonely and wished you could have been more confident like the other children but instead had just felt jealous of them. And as you grew up, your jealousy worsened. People around you started to get into relationships with one another and you felt excluded from it all, even more so when couples married and settled down. Years later, and still single, you pluck up the courage to go to a party, thinking you might meet someone there. Susie, a member of your group, is confident, sociable and witty, has an attractive partner and, not surprisingly, is very popular. You are reminded of how you felt as a child. You feel increasingly jealous of this person and, before you know it, blurt out a mildly derogatory comment in her direction, one of the only things you have said all night. Understandably the couple distance themselves from you, as do the other people they are with.

Life's mental scars can accumulate and muddy the waters in numerous different ways but the consequence is always the same. Innocuous events trigger memories of an unpleasant emotional experience from the past. Unpleasant emotions come flooding back, influencing you with behaviour inappropriate to the situation. If you act in accordance with these emotions, you will effectively be responding to an event different from that which just happened, your subjective experience and not your objective experience. You will have misperceived the situation and acted wrongly.

Perception/Ultimate Reality

If someone gives a presentation to Betty and Dave, and Betty comes away feeling what the speaker said was positive, but Dave comes away feeling what the speaker said was negative, who is right? If, when questioned, the speaker says that he had intended his talk to be positive, and all subsequent audiences with him feel that his presentation is positive, what went wrong for Dave? Why did Dave think the presentation was negative?

Destructive emotions cause a gap between the way things appear and the way things are. Unlike constructive emotions, which generally allow an accurate perception of reality (although it is possible to put an overly positive slant on things), destructive emotions *always* skew your perception. As mentioned, in the grip of a destructive emotion, feelings irrelevant to what is happening will influence your behaviour, but this is not all. Scientists have discovered that our emotional state preceding a visual perception actually influences what we see as well as our ability to think. My first driving lesson is a good example of these two impairments. Everything started off well. I was taken to a quiet local industrial estate and felt comfortable with the basics: clutch control, gears, steering and so on. But things went awry on the main road. As I drove out of the estate and into traffic, I felt my anxiety level shoot up. My hands tightened on the steering wheel and everything I had just learned seemed to evaporate. The driving instructor reminded me to periodically check my rear view mirror. I did this, but I could not actually see anything in the mirror. I could neither see clearly nor think clearly.

Emotions, like anxiety, can take us over for a moment. I am sure at some stage you too have experienced being angry, upset or anxious whilst trying to complete a task and thinking, 'I just can't think straight!' Negative emotions distort our perception, and each in its own characteristic way. For example desire will not let us see a balance between the pleasant and unpleasant (or constructive and destructive) qualities in something or someone. It can cause us to see things as perhaps 100% attractive. The more we imagine the focus of our desire in our minds, and the more positive spin we impose on that image, the more it affects our perception when we actually see the person or thing. Similarly, aversion blinds us to the positive qualities of something or someone. It can make us 100% negative regardless of how good it or they are in real life. Anger, one of the most powerful emotions, leads to people seeing only bad in everything. There is no point trying to reason with anyone who is angry because their reason will not return until they have calmed down.

Moods (which as we have said are drawn-out emotions) also impair our perception. Someone may start the day in a good mood and be perfectly amiable, but by the end of the day, when their mood has deteriorated, be biting people's heads off.

Dave perceived the positive presentation as negative because either (a) he was in a bad mood or (b) something about the speaker, or what he said, triggered one or more destructive emotions. Either way, Dave's perception of the presentation was wrong, and if our perception is wrong then we cannot conduct ourselves correctly. Only when our minds our calm, balanced and free from destructive emotions and negative moods do we see things the way they really are.

Extreme Behaviour

Everything covered so far applies to us all. Destructive emotions and negative moods distort perception and lead to disharmonious behaviour. They are the cause of unnecessary disputes between families, friends, work colleagues and perhaps even nations. But what is it that makes a minority of people so extreme? Many of us may fall out with each other from time to time, but there is a big jump from this to those committing violent crimes. We will now look at two types of violent criminal, Extreme 1 and Extreme 2, and the reasons why they may end up the way that they do. There is an important difference between these two examples that I would like to highlight. In Extreme 2, the primary focus is on the deficient upbringing of a child, where the finger of blame points firmly in the direction of the parents or guardians of the child. In Extreme 1 this is not the case. Some children brought up in stable, loving family environments still, nonetheless, end up living disharmonious lifestyles. Certain personality traits, combined with peer pressure, may, for example, lead an individual to experiment with heroin. The fantastically addictive nature of this drug can then rapidly lead the individual into crime or prostitution. In short, there is only so much that parents can do. Probably the best that can be done to avoid our children engaging in disharmonious lifestyles is for us to be aware of how they spend their time. What friends are they hanging out with? What interests do they have? Etc. If we are worried by our findings, we must do whatever we can to help but only first by employing caution and an abundance of love.

Unfortunately, parents who are deficient invariably say they have done everything they could for their children and apportion no blame at all on themselves, leading to generally good parents being branded deficient and the sole cause of their child's wrongdoing!

Extreme 1: Cultivating Aggression

We have spoken about how changing our behaviour changes the wiring in our brain and subsequently the thoughts and emotions we experience. If, for whatever reason, we choose to adopt disharmonious behaviour, we will eventually develop disharmonious thoughts and emotions. When I was about 12 there was a lad in my class who was shy, placid, politely spoken, and most definitely not in any way aggressive. We went on to different schools at the end of that year and I did not see him anymore until aged 18 when I was out for a drink with friends. A very rowdy group stumbled into the bar, knocking into tables and shouting expletives every other word. A friend of mine pointed out this lad was part of the group, that since we had known him he had got in with the wrong crowd, and that he had been in trouble with the police for theft and violence. Whilst ordering some drinks a little later our paths crossed and we exchanged a few words with him; it was like talking to a different person. His speaking style was completely different, loud and aggressive like he had been brought up by inmates of a prison. But the thing that most struck me was his face. Obviously he was six years older now, but his face was like that of someone else's, contorted, scowling and full of anger. He had staring, predatory eyes like windows into his troubled mind. How on earth could someone change so radically?

I believe our old friend's natural shyness, juxtaposed with the people he fell in with, led to him developing aggressive behaviour to mask his shyness and ingratiate him with the group. I do not believe he was any more a victim of destructive emotions than you or I when he was 12 years old. Instead, I think that his repeated bad behaviour gradually rewired his brain, increasing destructive emotions and negative moods over the years. He became the person he initially just pretended to be. His face was no act; it was a reflection of what he now truly felt inside. And of course this may have all been compounded by alcohol and/or drug abuse. Research has found that the brains of people under 18 are particularly sensitive; fundamental wiring is still underway and can be irreversibly changed. Excessive alcohol has been shown in youngsters to lead to a permanent reduction in concentration and psychoactive drugs, such as marijuana and LSD, can lead to schizophrenia. Alcohol and drug abuse alone can change a person's personality.

This is what I would call a kind of everyday example of how someone can become aggressive. The deliberate cultivation of aggression can, however, take a much more serious form. Terrorist organisations are known to deliberately cultivate individuals' hate and aggression whilst discouraging the positive qualities: compassion, love and empathy. In some instances, games are played whereby trainees are awarded points for animals that they kill. The larger the animal killed, the more points they receive. To further quash positive emotion, fighters may be told (if a religious-based organisation) that yearning to be home with loved ones during combat is in fact the Devil enticing them away from God's work.

In the previous chapter we saw that if we modify our behaviour and train ourselves to be good, we will be happier. Alternatively, we can if we choose train ourselves to be bad, but if we do it is at the expense of our happiness.

Extreme 2: Criminal Psychopaths

NB. For simplicity, I did not want to differentiate between psychopath and sociopath. I believe psychopath has more resonance with people so I have used it as a blanket term.

Immanuel Kant believed that we do not have to learn what is right and wrong, it is an innate attribute of the mind; morals are based solely on reason. I believe he was partially right and partially wrong. I believe he was wrong in that morals (in my view) are based both on reason and emotion, but right in that because emotions are inherent in the mind, they instinctively guide us towards the right course of behaviour.

The operative word here is inherent which means, 'essentially in'. For most of us, emotions regulate what we do and the level to which we do it, but for a minority of people this is not the case.

Humans are born with a will to survive and a will to procreate. In addition to this, and like some animals, humans are also born with the seeds of compassion, love, kindness and empathy. These seeds must be nurtured during infancy if they are to flourish. If they are neglected, they can remain underdeveloped or, worse still, be extinguished entirely from our emotional repertoire.

Daniel Stern, whilst a psychiatrist at Cornell University School of Medicine, discovered a relationship between infant and parent which he called attunement. Attunement is when parents ensure that their infant has the reassuring feeling of being emotionally connected to them, affirming messages which indicate that they know how the infant is feeling. For example, a baby squeals with delight and the mother affirms that delight by giving the baby a gentle shake, cooing, or matching the pitch of her voice to the baby's squeal. If parents consistently fail to show any empathy with an emotion, the child starts to avoid expressing, and probably feeling, that emotion. It is imperative that children, particularly between 0-3 years, are brought up in a caring, loving, harmonious environment if their emotions are to be wired up correctly. If not, it is possible that when the child reaches adulthood, she may never experience certain emotions.

In the most severe cases where many emotions have failed to wire up, individuals may be left with their base feelings only, namely a will to survive (fear, anger and happiness) and a will to procreate (desire). As a consequence, such individuals are entirely selfish. When exposed to acts of kindness they are likely to perceive the situation as merely an opportunity from which they can gain something for themselves. Psychopaths lack empathy and compassion. They are devoid of conscience and have no qualms or remorse about committing the most atrocious acts.

Most of us find this very difficult to relate to. How could anyone commit murder and not feel anything for the victim or the victim's loved ones? To try and understand this, imagine that I asked you to deliberately smash a glass outside on a path. Imagine for a moment smashing the glass and then consider how you would feel afterwards. I doubt you would feel very upset or remorseful. I suspect, if anything, you may actually feel quite exhilarated, a rush of adrenaline, or perhaps even that it was a cathartic exercise! This is exactly the kind of terminology psychopaths use when asked to describe their feelings when killing someone. It is very disturbing, but to individuals devoid of empathy and compassion, 'smashing' a human being is no different to smashing a glass.

Psychopaths typically never perform any action unless believing in some way that it is beneficial to them and often they employ manipulative techniques (such as charm) to get what they want. Surprisingly, it is estimated perhaps as many as 1% of the population are psychopaths. Fortunately, only a small fraction of this 1% become criminal psychopaths with others sometimes using their disposition to do well in areas such as business.

Quite what causes a small percentage of psychopaths to become criminal is unclear, but other aspects of their upbringing seem likely factors. How we are brought up is a very important influence on us all. Children are programmed to love and trust their parents wholeheartedly. If that trust is violated, say by violence, emotional abuse or sexual abuse, how is a child disposed to ever trust and love anyone again? Such treatment cultivates any number of powerful and long lasting destructive emotions. It says to children that violence or sexual misconduct is okay, that this behaviour is perfectly acceptable. The community is another factor. If children grow up and see violence all around them they will believe it is normal, and when bad behaviour is rewarded by guardians or peers, they will believe not only that it is normal but that it is desirable.

Following is a summary of *some* of the key factors which lead to the most extreme criminals. Clearly, if we can address these factors, we can begin to make inroads into building a more harmonious society.

NB.   The true or primary psychopath does not experience fear which suggests a biological abnormality. True psychopaths do not improve with any known treatment methods.

The Path to Becoming an Extreme and Violent Individual

- *A baby boy is born with a will to survive, a will to procreate and the seeds of love, compassion, kindness and empathy.*
- *Between 0-3 years these seeds are not cultivated; as a consequence he may never experience these essential regulatory qualities.*
- *One or more parent is violent towards him. An array of destructive emotions and resentment builds up including anger, hate, fear and a feeling of inferiority. He learns that violence is acceptable behaviour.*
- *He is not appropriately disciplined from a young age.*
- *His friends and community exhibit violent and other disharmonious behaviour.*
- *He grows to believe that violence is not only acceptable but gets you what you want and wins you respect amongst your peers.*

- *As he practices aggression and violence, these traits become increasingly hard wired. When he indulges in acts which should generate positive emotions, he feels no more than an adrenaline rush.*
- *His main sources of happiness are alcohol, drugs, sex, and the adrenaline rush from violent crime.*

The Behavioural Regulator

Emotions are the single most important requirement in regulating behaviour. They determine whether we perceive situations clearly and conduct ourselves properly and they prevent people from engaging in barbaric crime. When our emotions are stable and in harmony, we conduct ourselves humanely no matter what our political or religious persuasion. Without the key positive emotions we are little more than biological machines; relationships are hollow and meaningless, life is cold and dull.

The British Prime Minister Tony Blair famously said that his three main priorities were, 'Education, education, education'. Personally, I believe that the three main priorities for a harmonious society are:

Emotion, emotion, emotion.

The Londoner's assailants in the opening paragraph were both from broken homes and were both users of cannabis.

Emotional, Social and Philosophical Education

We must not only educate our children, we must *emotionally educate* them too. As the previous chapter hopefully demonstrated, nothing has more sway on behaviour, and therefore the stability of a society, than the emotions of the individuals who constitute the society. Children must be brought up in loving, compassionate, empathic environments if they are to learn these essential regulatory qualities.

Many countries tackle criminality in the same way as the UK: offenders are locked up and 'rehabilitated' before they rejoin the community. Year-on-year around 50% of released prisoners in England and Wales re-offend at an estimated cost to the taxpayer of £10bn per year. The most dangerous offenders, criminal psychopaths, require permanent incarceration. When you consider this staggering cost, overcrowded prisons and, worst of all, the devastation and heartache caused by criminal and terrorist activity, the urgency for a more effective solution is clear.

Most people agree that in all walks of life prevention is better than cure. How individuals turn out is no exception, rehabilitating offenders is infinitely harder and less effective than ensuring the correct upbringing of a child. Because of this, I personally believe in developing our current methods of postnatal care. If children's emotional development were monitored, particularly between the ages of 0-5 years, parents could be given advice if there were any signs of abnormality. In cases of serious emotional deficiency, children could undergo specialist treatment. The financial cost I believe would be significantly less and the benefit to society potentially huge. (Of course careful research should be undertaken to establish the most effective, and least invasive, method for monitoring children's emotional development.)

In addition, there is mounting evidence against children under three years old spending large periods of time in nurseries. The behaviour of children who do can become disruptive, perhaps due to them vying for the attention of frequently young and poorly qualified staff. Governments should value good parenting and do everything possible to promote and support this over nursery care.

Psychologist Steve Biddulph's book, 'Raising Babies', provides detailed information on the effects of nursery on the under threes.

Parents and teachers alike can improve a child's emotional and academic intelligence by creating a happy, loving environment where learning is fun. Tests have shown that pupils retain information better simply by teachers smiling more often and when the emphasis is on rewarding good behaviour and performance instead of punishment. (And it is proven that happier children make happier adults.)

Montessori schools and the Swedish Kunskapsskolan (the knowledge school) are proving excellent models for a new approach to education. Both cultivate children's self esteem, confidence and a love of learning by allowing a high degree of freedom and self development. The 'leaner-centric' (as opposed to 'teacher-centric') approach gives rise to individuals who view life as an exciting adventure, full of possibilities. Some schools in the USA, and now also England, Australia and the Netherlands, are pioneering a program called PATHS (Promoting Alternative Thinking Strategies). As well as learning the three Rs, the PATHS curriculum ensures that children learn to be aware of theirs and others' emotions, together with techniques for managing their emotions. This is an excellent idea which I hope we see grow in popularity. Emotions are so important and they should be nurtured both at home and at school. (*Information on the PATHS curriculum can be obtained from http://www.channing-bete.com/ prevention-programs/paths/paths.html.*)

In the course of the day, children are exposed to a lot of negative teaching in the form of computer games, television, films, music and books. To counter this, emotional education should be supplemented with social education which makes clear, among other social issues, that such media depict a fantasy world. Adolescents in particular must understand that there is nothing brave or cool about negative emotions or anti-social and violent behaviour.

Juvenile delinquents often talk of respect, how committing offences such as violent crime wins them respect from their peers, how their victim disrespected them. It should be emphasised to children that 99% of the population utterly *disrespect* violent people, that violence is seen by most as ignorant and animalistic. Shaming and humiliation are effective deterrents. For example, it could be pointed out that you are forced to speculate what other animalistic behaviour a violent individual engages in: do they defecate outdoors and wipe their bottoms on the ground (children relate to toilet humour and this is a suitably uncool image)? It must be explained that violence and sex crimes are among the most intolerable behaviour. Words such as primitive and embarrassing used to dissuade youth from believing them in some way respectable. We must underline that there is nothing heroic or brave about losing control of yourself and that there is no place in a modern human society for immature baboons.

Some men think that to openly express love, compassion and even happiness (particularly in the form of enthusiasm), is a sign of weakness. Social education must dispel this fallacy. Boys should be taught that there is a big difference between someone who is *confident* and someone who is a thug or has no feelings. Confidence is an attractive quality, a man with no feelings on the other hand is about as attractive to women as a baboon (and baboons have feelings!). Children must learn that emotional intelligence is what differentiates us from animals, that people who exhibit compassion and love towards all living things, and who exude confidence and self-control in difficult situations, are the people we should respect. Positive emotions should be encouraged. We must explain that they are what give all the flavour to life, what can turn a casual acquaintance into a lifelong friend. People who do not embrace positive emotions are dead to the world, biological machines failing to understand the true nature of their existence, and getting little out of life as a result. We must ensure our children understand that, despite what they may watch at the cinema, positive emotions are cool and negative emotions are uncool.

I believe Aristotle was correct when he said, '*the fate of empires depends on the education of the youth*'. If we are to ensure a harmonious society, we must ensure that we educate our children to be harmonious individuals. By adulthood, people become set in their ways, resilient, and frightened sometimes of change. In contrast, children's minds are like sponges, soaking up all that they are exposed to. We must provide them with an academic education but also an emotional and social education. We must teach them the core basic philosophies; philosophies such as '*treat others as you would like others to treat you*', '*do not take revenge or return aggression in arguments (love thy enemy)*' and '*do not tar people with the same brush*'. We must teach children that being selfish and insular leads to unhappiness. We must teach children that superiority does not equal happiness. We must teach children humility. And we must teach children to seek out their own understanding, not blindly accept what they are told.

Faith schools arguably focus more attention on core philosophies but are not conducive to social integration (the segregation of Catholic and Protestant pupils in Northern Ireland is testimony of this, as too is the success of the newly formed integrated schools). Ideally, emotional, social and philosophical education should be taught in fully integrated schools, together with information on all the world religions. I believe many pupils are generally interested in different faiths and would benefit greatly from mixed-faith schools. In-depth study of any one religion, in my view, should be extra-curricular until age 16.

How
to be
Human

The Heart of Humanity

In the aftermath of the Asian tsunami in December 2004, we were reminded of two very important things. Firstly, each and every one of us can help to improve the world in which we live, we do not have to sit back and leave it all to the politicians (many of whom are more concerned about staying in power, or getting in power, than the long-term future of society or the planet). Secondly, we were reminded that we are all human beings, and that all human beings share the same basic desire: to be happy and free from suffering. We should always view people from this standpoint.

Enemies are made when we act in isolation, when we do not see ourselves as part of the group, society, country or world community of which we are all respectively a part. The tsunami dissolved insularity. It lifted our masks and revealed, temporarily at least, that humans are in this life thing together. It reminded us that individually we are vulnerable but collectively we are strong, that positive emotions (love and compassion) bind us together, and negative emotions (anger, desire and jealousy) drive us apart.

Both animals and humans alike experience positive and negative emotions.

Humans differ in that we possess the faculty of negotiation and we can develop our emotional intelligence to avoid acting impulsively. Lacking these qualities, animals have little choice but to use aggression and violence to solve disputes. We could say, therefore, that it is these two things which differentiate us from animals. Put another way, we could say that the *heart of humanity* (the characteristics of being human) can be defined as:

To be human, be good.

People who actively mean to harm or kill others lack the heart of humanity. Behaviourally at least, they are not human.

Biologically speaking, humans, just like all other organisms, have two main objectives: to stay alive and reproduce. Nature gave us emotions to help meet these objectives, to guide us towards the best course of behaviour in different situations. Negative emotions, such as anger and fear, protect us; they are required for fight-or-flight responses to an emergency or threat. However, unlike animals, we should only act upon these to get ourselves or others out of danger; the disharmonious behaviour they cause is detrimental at other times. Positive emotions, such as love and compassion, operate at the other end of the spectrum. These lead to harmonious nurturing behaviour and benefit humans in two ways. Firstly, they ensure the intimate and vital bond between parent and infant, without which babies may not survive. Secondly, and as the tsunami demonstrated, they encourage us in adulthood to look after one another. If I look after you and you look after me it is a win-win situation; we improve each other's chance of survival. Love, compassion and empathy extended out from the family and drove us to embrace larger families. Members of harmonious communities and societies maximise their chance of survival and their quality of life.

Happiness, I believe, is an overall measure of how well we are physically and mentally faring, guiding us towards behaviour conducive to our survival. For example, compassion and love flood us with the desire to help, to offer the hand of friendship to those who are suffering. If we improve someone else's chance of survival, we increase the chance of them being around in the future should we need any help. Compassionate and loving acts therefore improve our chance of survival in the long run and, I believe, increase our happyometer reading to encourage this behaviour. Anger and hatred lead to physical conflict. Unless we our protecting ourselves or others they put us in danger, generate enemies and diminish our chance of survival. I believe to discourage repetitions of this behaviour, our happyometer reading decreases.

As discussed in the Happiness chapter, to increase our day-to-day feeling of happiness we must cultivate our harmonious thoughts, emotions and behaviour and diminish our disharmonious thoughts, emotions and behaviour. We can concisely summarise this as:

To be happy, be good.

NB. I believe our happyometer reading changes after, rather than during, harmonious/disharmonious behaviour.

*The objective of How to be Human is to answer the question, '**At the simplest level, what is the best way for human beings to conduct themselves?**' Combining the philosophy, 'to be happy, be good', with the heart of humanity derived in this chapter, 'to be human, be good', we arrive at the following answer:*

To be human and happy, be good.

Spirituality

We all want to be happy and we all want to get the very most out of our time in this world. Many people jump straight into life without giving things too much thought, until perhaps the autumn of their years when some revert to the natural philosophers they we were as children. Would it not be better to become philosophers of life right now, to nurture our childhood faculty of wonder, and enjoy every waking moment of every day?

> *What is this life if, full of care,*
> *We have no time to stand and stare.*
>
> *No time to stand beneath the boughs,*
> *And stare as long as sheep or cows.*
>
> *No time to see, when woods we pass,*
> *Where squirrels hide their nuts in grass.*

No time to see, in broad daylight,
Streams full of stars, like skies at night.

No time to turn to Beauty's glance,
And watch her feet, how they dance.

No time to wait till her mouth can,
Enrich that smile her eyes began.

A poor life this if, full of care,
We have no time to stand and stare.

'*Leisure*', by William Henry Davies, goes a long way in saying what I would like to try to get across in this chapter. Only when we lift our heads from whatever it is we spend our days doing, take a step back, and see the overall picture of which we are a part, can we put life into perspective. Only then can we discern answers to questions such as, 'Am I living my life the best possible way?' and, 'Is my day-to-day conduct acceptable?'

Having arrived at the philosophy, '*To be human and happy, be good*', what now? How exactly can we implement being good?

I believe the best way of approaching this philosophy is holistically, as a part of a bigger exercise and one which can probably best be described as, '*cultivating your spirituality*'. This final chapter is intended to be a practical one in which we look at how this can be done. Once we have covered the groundwork we will focus our attention on some simple exercises which, when incorporated into the day, will not only make your life more fulfilled, but increase your health and happiness. A consequence of increasing your spirituality is becoming a nicer, 'more good' and, therefore, happier person.

Changing Your Mind

I think everyone agrees that you can't enjoy your life to the full and be completely happy when you are physically unfit or unwell. Good health is a prerequisite for happiness; many people are accustomed to eating healthily and taking regular exercise. But what about the mind, the wiring in our brain responsible for how we see the world, what we think, and how happy we are? Most people just let their mind get on with things. Rarely do people take much notice of it unless something goes wrong, as in the case of developing a neurosis like anxiety, depression or a destructive emotion. At such times one may seek the help of a counsellor or psychiatrist, someone who can help iron out the disharmony in the mind.

Recently there has been something of a revolution in psychiatry. Research has shown that if we practise cultivating harmonious mental states, positive emotions such as compassion and love, we can immunise ourselves against developing destructive emotions and other mental afflictions (a philosophy expounded by the Dalai Lama). Prevention, as always, is more effective than cure. In addition to this, and as we saw in the 'Happiness' chapter, cultivating harmonious mental states both increases the effectiveness of the immune system and makes us happier. Physically working out keeps us physically healthy, and mentally working out keeps us mentally healthy (and contributes towards our overall physical health).

The reason we think the way we think, and behave the way we behave is due to the *current* wiring in our brain (something I personally like to refer to as our mind).

Everything we do in life shapes this wiring, everything we learn, and everyone we interact with. But something we should feel excited and optimistic about is that each of us has the capacity to rewire our brain, to take control and manage future wiring projects. We can, quite literally, change our mind.

What is Spirituality?

As we get older and become used to the routine, one could even say the monotony of living, many start to feel that life is hollow, that it lacks meaning or is missing something. Frequently, those who feel like this turn to religion; the main faiths have strong philosophical and spiritual components that help people to plug the gap. For many, religion and spirituality are inextricably linked. Personally, however, I see spirituality as something which, although taught as part of religion, is not inseparable from religion, a way of being that anyone can adopt if they want to (equally God and being good are not, in my view, inseparable from religion). So what exactly is it?

We have seen that our universe consists of systems within systems. From the unimaginably tiny to the unimaginably huge, everything is but part of something bigger. Everything is interconnected with everything else and nothing happens in isolation. We have seen that the longevity of these systems, both animate and inanimate alike, are governed by a Natural Law. Harmonious systems survive and perform well, disharmonious systems do not. For me, spirituality means acknowledging that you are a part of this overall picture. I see it as the active desire to integrate with everything around you, all living things, your environment and the universe, as harmoniously as possible. I believe it is understanding that only by so doing will you maximise your health, happiness and a long life. My personal definition of spirituality can therefore be summarised as follows:

Spirituality: *Awareness of being part of an interconnected universe and understanding that harmony with the universe improves health and happiness.*

If you believe in God you may prefer to consider spirituality to be more about connecting with God.

In the expression '*To be human and happy, be good*' we could replace the '*be good*' part with '*be harmonious*', as being good and being harmonious are one and the same thing. Being harmonious means adopting harmonious behaviour, emotions and thoughts (where behaviour <=> thoughts and emotions => happiness and health). My definition of cultivating your spirituality is the practice of increasing your harmony with all of creation. This can be achieved with the mental equivalent of a physical work out, exercises undertaken to rewire the brain, and, consequently, improve your health and happiness. Let us take a look at two techniques for changing your mind, for cultivating your spirituality and becoming healthier and happier as a result:

Cognitive Behaviour: Change your behaviour, and your thoughts and emotions will follow

Repeated behaviour changes the wiring in the brain. Learning to play an instrument is an excellent example; the brains of people who have spent many hours practising show increased wiring in the areas that deal with physical dexterity. Psychiatrists make use of this phenomenon to treat suffers of various mental disorders. Cognitive Behavioural Therapy (CBT) works by getting patients to practise changing their behaviour until eventually their thoughts and emotions change in sympathy with the new behaviour. We can employ this technique in cultivating our spirituality. By adopting more harmonious behaviour, we change the wiring in the brain and increase the number of harmonious thoughts and emotions we have. The more harmonious thoughts and emotions we have, the better our health, the greater our happiness, and the longer our life expectancy. Probably the simplest proven example of change your actions and your thoughts will follow is the act of smiling. Scientists discovered that when you force yourself to smile, the brain registers a slight increase in happiness.

The relationship between our behaviour and happiness, health and longevity can be summarised with the happyometer diagram:

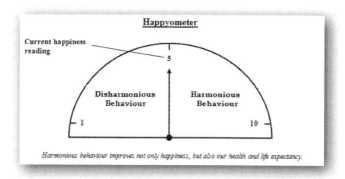

Harmonious behaviour improves not only happiness, but also our health and life expectancy.

CBT is also used to directly target negative ways of thinking. For example, a friend doesn't telephone or sends a seemingly curt email and you convince yourself that they no longer like you. A few days later your friend pops round, apologises, and explains they have had to work late all week whilst also managing some personal problems. Negative thinking left unchallenged can spiral out of control. CBT can be used to equip people with a suitcase of thought processes to apply in different situations e.g. 'My friend cares about me and would never deliberately upset me'. Techniques such as this ensure disharmonious thoughts are replaced with harmonious ones (and that our happyometer readings remain intact).

Meditation: Change your thoughts and emotions, and your behaviour will follow

Repeated behaviour changes the wiring in the brain, and that behaviour can be mental as well as physical. If you repeatedly have the same thought, you will reinforce the wiring in the brain associated with that thought, i.e. the thought becomes more prevalent in the mind. This is an important factor in addictions, say for example somebody who is obsessed with sex. The more the addiction is fed by thoughts associated with it (sexual imagery, fantasies or whatever), the worse it becomes. Meditation centres on this principle but its primary use is in cultivating harmonious thoughts, emotions and ultimately a harmonious mind. In the last part of this chapter, 'Cultivating your Spirituality', we look at meditations to cultivate our compassion, an exercise which in turn increases our happyometer reading. But until then, let us familiarise ourselves with the basics.

Many people are mistaken about what meditation is and can be put off when they find out. The important thing to note is that it is not an effortless exercise; it is *not* just merely relaxing. There are several different types of meditation but essentially it can probably best be described as consisting of two parts:

1) **Being relaxed.**
2) **Being mentally focused on just *one* thing. (Not daydreaming.)**

The way to think about meditation is like physical exercise. Why do we go to the gym or run, walk, or go swimming, or at least think that we should? These things all require our time and effort but we do them because we know we will feel healthier, look better, and ultimately be happier as a result. Meditation is very much of this ilk. It too takes a degree of time and effort but has many benefits, some of which include better health, enhanced concentration, and increased happiness. We are obsessed about keeping our bodies in check but place little importance on the brain. This is odd when you consider that our mind is solely responsible for what we think, say, do and feel.

Meditating regularly increases your enjoyment of life. For example, when out socially, or on holiday, it ensures that you are more focused on the moment and that you get as much out of everything as possible, rather than worrying about past or future events. And, unlike going to the gym or needing special equipment, it can be done pretty much anywhere. Meditation requires nothing but the desire to do it.

Let us try two simple examples so you can see for yourself what it is all about. Before commencing, indeed before commencing any meditation, remind yourself what you will get out of the exercise:

> *Regularly meditating, like any other repeated behaviour, rewires your brain. It improves your health, concentration, happiness and overall enjoyment of life.*

Meditation 1: Sensory Meditation

Many meditation books start off with the old 'close your eyes and focus on your breathing' meditation. Personally, I believe this Sensory Meditation is more interesting and it can be done anywhere without people thinking you're weird. Read, and then try the following:

Imagine you are a space traveller who has just landed on this planet. You have stepped outside your spaceship to take your first look around and are so interested in everything that you stop daydreaming or thinking about anything else; there's too much to take in.

Try to make yourself comfortable and relax. Perhaps take a few deep breaths and shake off any tension in your body.

Stop all your thoughts.
Turn off your internal voice and your internal jukebox (if, like me, you have songs going round in your head a lot of the time).

Focus on your hearing only, as if you are listening out for something. (If the internal voice returns, or the internal jukebox starts up, listen more intently, it will help to curb it.)

Whilst still listening, look about at what's around you.

Now add in the sense of touch; what can you feel? (If you are outside, feel the air moving over you.)

Add in the sense of smell; what can you smell?
Focus solely on what you can experience through your senses, and shift your attention between them.

See how long you can operate in sensory mode only, keeping your thoughts, internal voice, and internal jukebox at bay. Many people who try this for the first time only manage about 30 seconds before an extraneous thought pops into their mind, but with practise you will become better.

This meditation calms your mind and increases your concentration. It may sound new age, but there is something generally spiritual that you feel when practising it, particularly in quiet, idyllic, picturesque environments (for instance a candlelit cathedral). Try it now before reading on.

Meditation 2: Just Watching Meditation.

Try to make yourself comfortable and relax. Again take a few deep breaths and shake off any tension in your body.

Turn off the internal voice and the internal jukebox.

Let visual thoughts only occur naturally, but do not process them. Instead, just watch them dissolve away.

This meditation can be used in conjunction with the previous one to tackle any thoughts as they arise. It is also useful when you have a lot of stuff going on internally and you wish to calm your mind, particularly when trying to get off to sleep. Try it now, before reading on.

Cultivating Your Spirituality

To be as healthy and happy as possible, and to get as much out of life as possible, you must be good and a way to ensure that you are good is by cultivating your spirituality. Cultivating your spirituality can be thought of as an exercise to become as harmonious (good) as possible. It involves developing harmonious emotions, thoughts and behaviour which in turn increases harmony with those around you and the universe of which you are a part.

Everything we do wires our brain. Things that we do often become increasingly hardwired, more entrenched in our personalities. Following are some spiritual exercises which, if repeated, will rewire your brain and cultivate your spirituality. The Morning Mantras encapsulate the essence of the whole book and the more deeply ingrained these are the better. The other meditations and exercises help to develop your spirituality further, the more they are repeated the more a part of you they will become.

Every second that passes is a second less that we'll be a part of this world. We must not delay in our spiritual evolution.

Exercise 1: Morning Mantras

01) The entire history of our universe was required so that you, your family, your friends, your work colleagues, and every living thing on this planet may exist now. Collectively this is our time; we are one overall family that exists together at this moment in history. Be aware of this today when you interact with other members of your collective family.

02) Everything you do has an effect. To enjoy your life to the full, and to be as healthy and happy as possible, you must be in harmony with yourself, those around you, all living things and your environment. Keep your happyometer in mind; harmonious emotions, thoughts and behaviour increase your health and happiness, disharmonious emotions, thoughts and behaviour decrease your health and happiness.

03) Treat others as you would like others to treat you. Treating people badly is an example of disharmonious behaviour that diminishes your health and happiness.

04) Anger is our enemy. Treat trying situations as a battle with this most destructive emotion, an exercise in increasing your patience and tolerance. To help keep calm, be aware of your emotions. **As soon as you notice the onset of anger**, nip it in the bud before it has the chance to grow (otherwise the energy generated will need an outlet). Take a deep breath and gather your composure or perhaps, if possible, take a break from the situation. Increasing your patience and tolerance increases your health and happiness. And remember, it is our ability to negotiate and our emotional intelligence which differentiates us from animals.

05) Problems are an integral part of living. Use each problem you encounter as an opportunity to improve the way you handle it.

Exercise 2: Imagination Meditation (The Gift of Consciousness)

Imagination meditations, as their name suggests, are ones where we focus our attention entirely on imagery, scenarios and stories that we create in our mind's eye. They are not the same as daydreams where the mind flits from thought to thought as they remain solely within the frame of the picture we create. They can be used to cultivate feelings, emotions, and to prepare for forthcoming events among many other things.

Make yourself comfortable and relax; take a few deep breaths and shake off any tension in your body.

Imagine making a robot out of Meccano or Lego. You give it a head, arms and legs, then, finally, it is finished. You stand up your robot to inspect it and to change its position, moving an arm here and a leg there. It has a basic humanoid appearance but is utterly lifeless, a cold ensemble of metal and plastic standing there on the table where you made it. On turning your robot around you find a small switch on its back. You have no idea how the switch got there or what it does so you flick it to see what happens. In an instant, the robot becomes conscious. It raises one of its hands and on inspecting it closely says, 'Who am I?' It then looks up at you and asks, 'Who are you?' and 'What am I doing here?' It has developed a sense of staring out from its own body.

Close your eyes for a few moments and then slowly open them again. Focus on your sense of awareness, the sense of staring out from your body that robots do not have. Raise and inspect one of your hands and then look at what you are conscious of around you. Touch something nearby, feel its texture.

Whenever you feel bored, repeat this meditation. Remind yourself of the incredible and magical Gift of Consciousness.

Exercise 3: Meditation (Sensory Meditation)
Follow up the previous meditation with the Sensory Meditation we covered earlier. You are a conscious being. You have the ability to sense, experience, and interact with your world on an emotional level:

Make yourself comfortable and relax; take a few deep breaths and shake off any tension in your body.

Stop all your thoughts.
Turn off your internal voice and internal jukebox.

Focus first on your hearing and then gradually introduce the other senses in succession.

Focus solely on what you can experience through your senses and shift your attention between them.

Practise extending the length of time you can stay purely in sensory mode, free from the clutter of thoughts.

The Sensory Meditation is a good one to practise when out for a walk.

Exercise 4: Live in the Moment Meditations
A meditation is really any time that you are relaxed and focused on just one thing. We feel at our happiest and operate

at our best when this is the case, when we are focused solely on the matter in hand, and not worrying about past or future events. '*Flow*' is the name used to describe this state, the times when we are 100% focused on whatever it is that we are doing.

Practise treating everyday events as meditations in their own right. For example, when next having a conversation with someone, try to focus 100% on what they are saying. See if you can develop your Emotional Intelligence. What emotion or mood is the other person feeling, particularly in light of what you say? What emotion and mood is their conversation inducing in you? This practise will ensure you make much closer and more meaningful connections with others.

When at parties and social gatherings, use the sensory meditation to soak up all the sights, sounds and smells of the occasion. You will enjoy yourself much more if you do and it will keep extraneous thoughts at bay.

When at work or engaged in chores about the house try to focus solely on what you are doing. If it is a menial task, become aware of the different sensations you are experiencing.

When listening to music, focus on all the nuances in sound; be aware of any emotions the music invokes in you.

In short, when you enjoy 'just being', you are engaged in a spiritual exercise.

Exercise 5: Cultivating Compassion Improves our Health and Happiness

Compassion is the wish that others may be free from suffering and the causes of any suffering. I believe that this positive nurturing emotion evolved in humans for two reasons:

1) To ensure that mothers bond with their children.
2) To ensure that we look after other members of our community so in turn they look after us. (Humans survive better in groups and have a better quality of life.)

When those around us are happy and surviving well, we too have a better chance of happiness and surviving well. We have a vested interest, therefore, to ensure other people's well-being, and happiness and compassion lead us to behaviour conducive to this. Nature rewards a compassionate act with an increase in our happyometer reading. I believe it does this to acknowledge we have indirectly improved our own chance of survival, and to encourage similar behaviour in future.

> *If we deliberately cultivate our compassion, we will be healthier and happier as a result. In addition, positive emotions, like compassion, ward off negative emotions.*

The key to the following meditations is feeling the emotions that you experience during them. Meditation 5.2 is not a pleasant one, but stick with it, and with regular practice your happyometer will steadily climb.

Exercise 5.1: Imagination Meditation on Compassion 1

When you see an animal in nature, be it a butterfly, bird, squirrel or whatever, remind yourself that this small creature has essentially the same feelings as you. It does not want to come to any harm, and cares for its young as we care for our young. It is unique and just happens to share its short existence with you. You could easily hurt or kill this creature, but intelligent, compassionate human beings occupy a privileged status in that we can help to look after all members of the animal kingdom.

Imagine watching the animal tenderly and gently nurturing its young. Allow your feelings for the animal's welfare to flourish.

Exercise 5.2: Imagination Meditation on Compassion 2

Survivors of World War I have told heart-wrenching stories about their fallen comrades. Many explained how they were with a friend when he died, how they offered him what little comfort they could in no man's land where he lay frightened and trembling. Often they said that in the last moments, their dying friend asked for his mother.

Imagine that you were in this position, embracing a lifelong friend or family member who has been seriously injured.

You recount happy times together when you were children, the things you got up to when you were growing up.

Your friend asks you to help him.

He asks for his mother.

He dies in your arms.

For as long as possible, focus on how you feel at each stage of this meditation.

Exercise 5.3: Imagination Meditation on Compassion/ Love 3

Babies quite naturally and effortlessly generate compassion in adults. Of course, nature made us this way to ensure that we bring up our young and secure the survival of the species. If you have a baby then you can skip this meditation (you will be getting enough first hand compassion/love experience!) If you do not, or if your children are grown up, try the following:

Imagine you have a young baby. He cannot feed or look after himself and is utterly dependent on you to look after him.
He looks up to you from his cot with big, round, bright eyes.
He smiles at you.
You pick him up and he nuzzles into your neck.
You put your face alongside his.
He snuffles contently in your ear.

Hold the feelings this meditation generates in mind.

Exercise 5.4: Cognitive Behaviour - Do things for others
If you deliberately engage in kind, thoughtful and compassionate acts, you will gradually experience more happiness. (There is much evidence that people involved in charitable work have increased their happiness as a result.) When you make other people feel better or happier, you will feel better and happier. (Change your actions and your thoughts and emotions will follow.) An easy place to start is giving a family member or friend a little of your time to take them out, treat them or to help with some of their chores. Asking others about their lives and sharing anecdotes is also simple and beneficial to both parties.

Exercise 5.5: Imagination Meditation on your own Suffering
Recall to yourself a time when you were unwell, or in pain or preferably both.

Relive in your mind how this felt.
Replay the discomfort, and how you yearned to be better.

When you encounter someone who is unwell, in pain, or perhaps just down on their luck and feeling unwell as a result, recall this meditation to yourself. Remember the Dalai Lama's philosophy when meeting anyone, '*This is another human being just like myself, and just like myself, they want to be happy and free from suffering*'. Always view people in this way. Nationality, gender, faith and sexuality are merely the hats that human beings wear.

Exercise 6: Imagination Meditation (Cherish your Loved Ones)

Bring a loved one to mind.
Recall your life with this person.
Imagine this person is no longer in your life.

Exercise 7: Imagination Meditation (Be Kind, Amiable and Thoughtful)

Recall someone you saw regularly (at school, work, socially etc.) who was unkind, unfriendly or behaved thoughtlessly towards you.

Remember the feelings you felt when they treated you the way that they did.

Bring this to mind if, for whatever reasons, you feel compelled to treat someone badly, or if perhaps you have not given thought to how your behaviour affects others. (We feel happier when we are patient and tolerant of even the most difficult people, and harmonious behaviour avoids conflict.)

Exercise 8: Have Fun!

On the surface you may consider this final exercise selfish, unspiritual and of no benefit to anyone other than you:

Take regular time out to pursue your personal interests and do them wholeheartedly.

As we get older and our responsibilities grow we can increasingly neglect to do the things we enjoy. The consequence, should you fall foul of this, is that you will become bitter, dissatisfied, less happy and, most importantly, less well equipped to be of benefit to others. The gift of life should be enjoyed so make regular time to get out there and enjoy it!

Deep down, all humans are the same

We all want to be happy and we all want to get the very most out of our time in this world. To do so we must make the overall picture of which we're a part the foundation of our day-to-day existence; life happens within the context of this picture.

We can only achieve optimum health and happiness by being a harmonious part of the picture. We can only do this by taking control of our mind, by practising exercises that wire our mind for health and happiness. If you want to improve your fitness you take regular physical exercise. If you want to improve your happiness you must take regular mental exercise. I believe cultivating your compassion, love, kindness and empathy (your goodness), or more succinctly, cultivating your spirituality, is a suitable name for this exercise. It could be said that happiness is a measure of how well we are physically and mentally or, if you prefer, physically and spiritually faring.

Happiness, love, compassion and kindness, are I believe, fundamental in our existence. If you consider your fondest memories, they will be times centred on these positive emotions, occasions when, no doubt, you were completely at one with the moment, or as Sweden's most successful export would say, '*Hav-ing, the, time, of, your, life*'. We often make a meal out of getting along with one another, but ultimately, deep down, all humans are the same. Ultimately, we want to party!

FURTHER READING

The main books influential in the writing of How to be Human and which I recommend for further reading were:

Destructive Emotions by Daniel Goleman

The Art of Happiness by the Dalai Lama & Howard C. Cutler

Emotional Intelligence by Daniel Goleman

Raising Babies (Should under 3s go to nursery?) by Steve Biddulph

The Tibetan Book of Living and Dying by Sogyal Rinpoche

Teach Yourself to Meditate by Eric Harrison

Sophie's World by Jostein Gaarder

Probability 1 by Amir Aczel

The Nicomachean Ethics by Aristotle

Rights of Man by Thomas Paine

The Age of Reason by Thomas Paine

Stuart Murray has studied and appreciated philosophy his entire life. When his son died from leukemia, he turned to philosophy and spirituality to cope with the tragic event. The ideas he has discovered are detailed in *How to Be Human*.

As a technical author, Murray writes instructional manuals for international companies. He lives with his wife and daughter in England.

Printed in Great Britain
by Amazon

41531790R00086